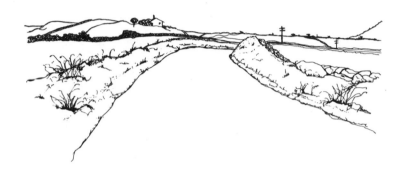

THE PIPES
ARE CALLING

THE PIPES
ARE CALLING

Our Jaunts Through Ireland

Niall Williams and
Christine Breen

Pen and ink drawings by Christine Breen

Excerpts from "Lines Written On a Seat on the Grand Canal, Dublin" and "Pegasus," from *The Collected Poems,* by Patrick Kavanaugh, © copyright 1972 by Patrick Kavanagh, reprinted by permission of Devin-Adair Publishers; excerpt from "In Gallarus Oratory" from *Poems, 1965–1975* by Seamus Heaney, copyright © 1966, 1969, 1972, 1975, 1980 by Seamus Heaney. Reprinted by permission of Farrar, Straus & Giroux (United States of America), and from *Door Into the Dark* by Seamus Heaney reprinted by permission of Faber & Faber Ltd., London; excerpt from *The Year In Ireland* by Kevin Danaher © 1972 by Kevin Danaher, reprinted by permission of The Mercier Press; excerpts from *A Visitor's Guide to the Dingle Peninsula,* by Steven MacDonogh © 1985 by Steven Mac-Donogh, reprinted by permission of Brandon Press; excerpt from *The Islandman,* by Thomas O Crohan (O Criomthain) translated by Robin Flower © 1937, by permission of Oxford University Press; excerpts from *The Blue Guide to Ireland,* © 1979, reprinted by permission of A & C Black (Publishers) Ltd.

Published in the United States of America by
Soho Press, Inc.
1 Union Square
New York, NY 10003

Library of Congress Cataloging-in-Publication Data

Williams, Niall, 1958–
The pipes are calling : our jaunts through Ireland / Niall
Williams & Christine Breen.
p. cm.
ISBN 0-939-149-33-8
1. Ireland—Description and travel—1981– 2. Northern Ireland—
Description and travel—1981– 3. Williams, Niall, 1958– —
Journeys. 4. Breen, Christine, 1954– Journeys. I. Breen,
Christine, 1954– . II. Title.
DA978.2.W55 1990
914.15'04824—dc20   89-26104 CIP

Book design and composition by The Sarabande Press

Manufactured in the United States of America

First Edition

This book is dedicated to Michael and Pauline, Lucy and Larry, Phyllis and Tommie, Mary, Joe, Francie, and Niamh, without whose help there would have been no jaunts.

AUTHORS' NOTE

Yet again, this book was written by two people. No episode belonged exclusively to either of us, whether in the living or the writing. Sections were drawn from both our journals and both of our pens have had a part in every page.

· Contents ·

ONE

New Year's day in Kiltumper—Bicycles to
Gortnaheera—Lounging in the Dunraven Arms,
Adare—Coursing in Clounanna

3

TWO

Conversations on a horse—A walk from Sandymount
Green into Viking Dublin—The spirit of Jonathan Swift
on a Liffey-gray afternoon

30

THREE

The Kingdom of Kerry—"Beware of Descending
Mist"—The View from the Dingle Peninsula—Roads
that were silver in the rain

47

FOUR

On the trail of the Cake Dance—Bunratty Folk Park or, a
sod of turf for the fire—Kilkenny, Ireland's medieval city

65

FIVE

'Road-housing'—A riding lesson—"I was looking for a
horse fair" in County Mayo—Knock Shrine—A search for
Moore Hall

87

SIX

The Ceili Mor at Cois na Habhna—Fleadh Nua in Ennis,
or dancing in the streets—The Hush of Inisheer—
Bicycling on an island

108

SEVEN

Summer is a fine season for long journeys—Cuil Aodha—
Kenmare, village of our courtship—Italian gardens on an
Irish island—A night in Bantry House

132

EIGHT

The road North—Newry—County Down—Belfast at
sunset—from the Glens of Antrim to Giant's Causeway

154

NINE

Conversation about a cuckoo—Afternoon tea—We lose a
tenner at the Galway Races—On to West Mayo—A goat is
crowned

177

TEN

From Kiltumper to Donegal—The magic of
Glencolumbkille—Trá—Home again, home again, jiggedy
jig

198

THE PIPES
ARE CALLING

· Chapter One ·

*New Year's day in Kiltumper—Bicycles to
Gortnaheera—Lounging in the Dunraven Arms,
Adare—Coursing in Clounanna*

It is a cold clear day at the year's end. In the big field behind
the house, our three cows and the black goat are standing in
a line on the crisp, frosted mud eating hay. From my
window I see their breath rising on the morning air. I look
up at the high fields of Kiltumper where earlier today I took
a winter's walk to the top of the hill. This spring will be our
fifth since moving from Manhattan to Ireland; this place—
Kiltumper Cottage, in Kilmihil, a village in County
Clare—is our home now.

The life Chris and I have come to know here is so much

more (and less) than the one we'd imagined. In Manhattan, before making our decision to move, we never expected such welcome and hospitality from our neighbors, and never anticipated that they would turn out to be such warm, characterful people filled with spirit and endurance. Nor did we suspect the million mood-weathers of Clare, the agonies, as well as the joys, of tilling and tending a garden on the westerly edges of Ireland, nor the real grief of emigration. We could not foresee the hush of winter, the hardships and poverty of the west, the stream of old men and women's funerals emptying cottages in the lonely hills. Neither, of course, had we known of the clamor of bird song at summer dawns, the song of the cuckoo, freshly laid eggs on a bed of hay, the unsteady gallop of a new calf, hay trams in the meadows, *ceili* music, and the giddy happiness of joining with our friends in the dancing of jigs. Now such things have become the actual components of that "Irish feeling" in search of which we had left the comforts of our urban lives in America to make new lives in Ireland. For both of us, in differing ways, it has been a "return" and a beginning.

Responses to our accounts of this new life have been dual. We have had encouragement and support from so many, who, I think, join with us vicariously in a spirit of hope that we may endure and find what we came to seek. But we have also heard that our enterprise is doomed: that in Ireland today the best is past, that this country is ruined, too commercialized, expensive, and altogether lacking in the old Irish humor and wit; that all is changing and will soon be utterly lost. We are told that the "Irish feeling" that drew us to Kiltumper Cottage, and which we have found here, alive and well, is only our fantasy. We have been viewed as deluded romantics, or worse.

I think of the dozens of places—and people—across the country that Chris and I hold dear and I wonder. Have we been blind to the true life of the country today, having experienced what is perhaps a rare warmth and generosity in our corner of West Clare?

When I put the question to Chris, her reaction was typical. "There's only one way to find out," she said.

So we made our plans. We would set out in search of the "Irish feeling" that for us has become synonomous with the faces and places of this island. We would find out for ourselves.

Chris's Journal

New Year's Day, 1989. It was still dark when I awoke this morning to the sounds of Deirdre happily chatting to her toys in her room downstairs. With my eyes closed I listened to her telling her white teddy bear to dance. I could hear her say, "hop two three, hop two three." (Yesterday, she'd watched Niall and me practicing our steps for a Clare set).

Listening to my child, the dancing master, instructing her

teddy, and humming a little tune to myself, I rose from our futon bed on the floor, climbed over Niall's sleeping form, and negotiated my way down the steep, narrow, hundred-year-old stairs that lead to our kitchen below. Blinking the sleep from my eyes I thought of what Phyllis, a neighbor and friend, had said the day before, "Beware of what you do on New Year's Day; you may be doing it every day for the rest of the year." I nearly retreated upstairs to seek refuge beneath the quilt again.

Deirdre was still chatting when I went to her and gathered her up in my arms. We left the warmth of her room, and came into the wintry-morning kitchen for breakfast. I had switched on the electric fire so the chill was gone from the air. I sat Deirdre in front of the window that faces south, overlooking the garden, and pointed up to the sky. A white quarter moon still hung on the disappearing darkness of the night and all during breakfast Deirdre looked up at it, watching the morning break into day. If only every morning could begin like this, I thought. What an auspicious way to start the New Year!

After lunch we set off for a New Year's Day bicycle ride. I had given Niall a mountain bike with a baby seat attached for Christmas; it was time to try it out. We were soon to set off in search of Ireland: A bicycle ride on the first day of the year in the hills behind us would start the new year off right.

Niall is a bit skeptical not only about the bike's eighteen gears but also about maneuvering these roads with "that contraption" on the back. Personally, I believe that with the purple color, the three times six gear changes, and the sturdy plastic seat (capable of supporting fifty pounds' worth of child) he's a wee bit shy of the *showiness* of the thing. I hopped onto my miserable little five-speed envying

Niall and longing for my birthday in April when I had been promised my mountain bike.

Like a child first learning to ride without training wheels, Niall was all nerves. Balancing on one foot he delicately placed his right foot on the pedal and pushed off. Wobbling down our drive and out onto our Kiltumper road, he pedaled away.

Within moments we left our townland of Kiltumper and entered Castlepark. Townlands are usually separated from each other by rivers or streams or, in most cases, trickles of brooks. To the visitor they may be entirely featureless, unless, of course, you travel with an Ordnance Survey Map and a local parish history book. Our neighboring townland of Castlepark bears the only name in the parish of Kilmihil that derives from English. There used to be a castle there, and it is even marked on the map, but nothing remains today except for a bit of wall.

Niall was managing easily and gracefully and we whizzed down Moran's hill, bicycled up Cahermurphy hill and past the National School, the site of the old thatched-roof schoolhouse where my grandfather was taught as a child. "It's marvelous!" Niall remarked, "I could drink a cup of tea and cycle up these hills at the same time." He turned around to Deirdre. "How's Deirdre? Is Deirdre good?"

"Good," she responded. "Where's Mommy?"

"Here I am," I shouted weakly as the distance between our two bikes increased; Niall was cycling away at a hundred revolutions a minute and whistling; I was fading fast.

"See you at the top," he said.

Away the twosome went up the hill with great ease. The "contraption" holding Deirdre was, in fact, not as awkward as we had anticipated. I hopped off my bike and pushed it and my unfit self the rest of the way up the hill into the townland of Cahermurphy. Wait until April, I muttered.

The road at the top of Cahermurphy joins the old road from Ennis to Cree. We turned right and headed toward Gortnaheera, which means "garden of the shepherds," cycling along one of the prettiest roads in the parish. The long, straight boreen gently slopes and rises on its way toward Mullagh on the left and Doo Lough on the right, traversing quiet bogland with a great expansive view of the Atlantic.

Six hundred feet above sea level we rested and showed Deirdre the ocean. From Gortnaheera you are supposed to be able to see seven parishes; we could see the cliffs of Kilkee, twenty miles away to the southwest, and George's Head, jutting out. Before us, straight ahead, was Mutton Island, where a thriving seaweed processing factory once operated. The island can be reached by curragh from Quilty. To the northwest lay the bustling town of Miltown Malbay and the now-abandoned turf-burning power station. The Aran Islands were clearly visible as was O'Brien's Tower at the Cliffs of Moher, all silhouetted against the ocean. Directly behind us to the northeast was Slieve Callan, which rises 1,284 feet above the Atlantic and was an imposing mountain from our humble vantage point.

It was an hour before sunset. Deirdre looked cold, but she was quiet and content and gazed about peacefully. We turned and headed back toward Kiltumper. Through my daughter's eyes I saw West Clare—her home, our home. Dogs, cats, hens, a donkey, day-old early calves, geese, white goats, brown cattle, and Friesians. Peace and bird song and the early green growth peeping out along the hedgerows and ditches. A five-mile cycle on country boreens, a nod to the farmers and countrywomen who stopped a moment to look at the three of us as we passed by, and we returned home to a Happy New Year, looking forward to our jaunts about Ireland.

Whoever said we travel to learn about ourselves was right. Packing the old blue Peugeot, I realized I had already learned much about us from the way we set out from here with Deirdre. What we threw or folded carefully into suitcases betrayed us: in Chris's last-minute preparations, and my ordered and planned packing, were the secrets of our natures. Chris was the truer adventurer; I needed to be weighed down with books, papers, a whole company of words to feel the comfort of another place become temporarily my home. I needed to fill the bare shelf with my books and sit in a comfortable chair. I packed those things from Deirdre's bedroom that I imagined she could not do without: her "Duck" that was a chicken, her "Man" that was a dog. And hastening through the house on the morning of departure, it began to seem to me that leaving was as important a part of the journey as arriving. Four years ago, in the first months of our life here, a three-day trip to Dublin had brought on feelings of guilt in me at our desertion of our puddled muddied townland in the grip of winter. Now, on a mild February Saturday drizzling with soft rain, I felt somewhat the same. Ridiculous as it may seem, on the morning of leaving Kiltumper, I looked out at the land itself as if it were a friend I was parting from.

These were my chores to perform before leaving: pile two bales of hay into the feeder over the back wall for the cows; cast a slow, careful eye over the cows as they crossed the mucked meadows to eat; pour a double mix of steaming mush for our four surprised hens; set out a bed of hay and cans of food in the middle of the cabin for Max, the cat; then a familiar walk down the Kiltumper road to exchange a word with Francie over the farmyard wall where he would already be working, washing, driving, feeding, forking, and mucking out around his father's cows. He asked if I'd fed our animals, and offered to come that afternoon to check on them. I was not to worry, he said, he'd take care of them for me. I knew he would. I vowed, as I walked back along the empty road in the rain, that from wherever we went I'd bring him more of the Legos he collected.

The packed Peugeot banged and backfired, the rusted windscreen wipers smudged the glass in a constant arc of muddied drizzle. In the glove compartment was a stash of fresh mandarin oranges, the slow peeling and deliberate eating of which has become the best distraction for our traveling child. "Mr. Duck" Williams lay in his seat next to her, nappies by the dozens were jammed along the back window next to my fifteen-year-old paperback copy of Yeats's poems. The whole car shuddered to life, at last we were off. We were going to Adare.

Ten miles beyond Ennis, we left behind the farms of the west, rocky or boggy fields, rushes in soft places, and mucky gaps where briars and brambles were thrashed back. It had been a mild, moist winter in the west and the broad, fat fields of Limerick were already greener-than-green beneath a glowering sky. The cattle had all been taken in from the fields we passed now; there were no puddles silvering among the grasses here; the long stone walls that rose and fell on the soft undulations of this land were even and unbroken. This was rich country compared to the place we had come from. The hushed potholed road we had rattled and banged away from had turned into the wide dual carriageway that brings cars to Limerick City past the towers and arches of Bunratty Castle where the Earls of Thomond resided.

In the center of Limerick City we turned west on the road for Killarney. But I drove out of Limerick without seeing another signpost. Chris reminded me, with a smile, that I had brought Yeats's poetry but no map. Well, I retorted, she was the one who had been to Adare.

"That was seventeen years ago! I think we just had tea there. It was my first ever day in Ireland."

Chris's first ever day in Ireland: She had told me about the beautiful weather, her first glimpse of a thatched roof, and her grandmother Kitty's only visit back to the country she had left as a girl. I had seen the photograph: grandmother, son, and granddaughter—three generations of American Irish, standing in a pretty little village street.

"All I remember is a long wall, yellow houses, and a lot of trees."

"Oak trees," I said. And when Chris looked at me in surprise, I explained, "Adare. Ath Dara, Ford of the Oak Tree. You see the blessings of a good Irish education."

At Patrickswell the road forked. To the left was Charleville and the pasturelands of the south Limerick countryside where Eamon De Valera was born. To the right the road to Killarney and, within a few miles, Adare.

Almost at once Chris spied the trees, and minutes after passing the fork in the road we were traveling along a high wall into the heart of Adare village.

"Adare, 550 inhabitants," Chris read from the Blue Guide, "an unusually neat village . . . preserving a few thatched cottages. . . . It stands on the River Maigue and is noted for its trees and for its monastic remains. Ancestrally associated with the O'Donovans and with the Fitzgeralds, Earls of Kildare, it is now presided over by the Earls of Dunraven, whose seat is Adare Manor."

"The Earls of Dunraven, you see?" I said, sounding the name for all its romance and mystery, and pointing to a painted coat of arms hanging out from a long yellow building at the roadside: The Dunraven Arms Hotel.

Rain was streaming down as we got out of the car, and while our rooms were being readied we set ourselves out on a couch in the great bay window of the lounge. Here, on thick green carpets in an atmosphere that made me think of a nineteenth-century gentlemen's club, men in boots and raincoats were holding drinks as they stood around a blazing coal fire talking of sport. That afternoon, the Irish rugby team was playing England in Dublin in a bid to win the Triple Crown, and at first I supposed they were talking of that. It was only later, as they moved down to the bar for fresh glasses, and a lady in red-rimmed glasses and mucked Wellingtons came in and joined them, urgently drawing out a green card and pen, that I got some idea of what was going on.

"What double? Evens."

"Oh jays, he went well though."

"Flew it sure."

"Is Crazy Lad still in?"

"He is."

A momentary pause, golden shots of whiskey were drunk down, and another rain-drenched figure in muddied shoes walked right into the conversation.

"Tom. Meedham was *bate*."

"He was," said Tom in a thick northern accent, "beat easy, too. Pint of Guinness there, John."

From his raincoat pocket Tom took out a grubby-looking green card and the stub of a pencil. Like everyone else there the lady in the red-rims seemed to know Tom too. They were all together in some way, spreading out from the bar now as three more men and two women came in, all holding green cards, all nodding to each other, taking up positions near the fire and telling each other how the going was tough.

"It's very greasy out there, Mary."

"Worse than last year."

"Did Smokey Blue go well, Tom?"

"She did."

"And she was hurting all year," said Red-Rims quite loudly to no one in particular, drawing a little chorus of appreciative, agreeing murmurs from the others.

By now, Deirdre had fully explored all corners of the lounge, and just in time, we were told our rooms were ready. The Dunraven Arms is one of those special, old-fashioned, and elegant smaller hotels that are dotted around Ireland. Less than half an hour from Limerick City we were in what seemed to be an old Irish manor lodge, a place out of the tales of masters and servants, lords and ladies, complete with roaring fires, deep chairs, and walls full of images of horses and hunting. Another Ireland was February-ing down here, but the sheets of rain that were pouring from iron skies were nothing when your feet were to the fire and a hot pot of tea with warm scones was coming from the kitchen. In the sleepy wet heart of winter we were offered a special kind of Irish hospitality. As Deirdre raced off to go up and down the winding carpeted stair a hundred times, I tested the springs of the bed and felt Kiltumper was miles and miles away.

By early afternoon the rain had faded into soft weather. The lounge had emptied itself as swiftly and mysteriously as it had filled, and the three of us headed out through the fabulous demesne of Adare Manor to find a pub at which to watch the rugby. In the grounds of the manor there were daffodils opening everywhere, and as a weak watery sun shone somewhere beyond the clouds, springtime was briefly imaginable once more. Deirdre rocked in her stroller urging forward speed. Adare Manor, up a long drive and behind high walls, suddenly revealed itself as a staggering gray building of imposing majesty, complete with lovely ordered gardens, trimmed dwarf hedges, stone steps, and high arched windows sparkling with the light of chandeliers. It has only recently been restored and opened as a hotel. Here, on 840 acres of manicured grounds is a castle-like inn with barrel-vaulted ceilings, fifteenth-century Flemish-carved doors, ornate marble fireplaces, and an air of grandeur. Just for a moment we went inside, turning the brass ring to open a great heavy wooden door and step into a brown, high-roofed receiving hall. Another massive door creaked under my hand and we stepped into the second area of reception, where in softest lamplight a lady was sitting upon an ancient high-backed chair at a heavy oak table. Stairs rose behind her. We passed into a great bright room with windows looking down over the formal gardens, alive with early spring bulbs and bordered by neatly trimmed conical-shaped conifers.

We walked out of the manor grounds. Stretching back from Adare Manor and Dunraven Arms, the village of Adare, a winner of the Tidy Town's Competition, maintains (perhaps a little self-consciously) its picture-postcard-like atmosphere with thatch roofed restaurants and antique shops. But on a winter's day its wide, quiet street held away the world.

At the top of the town we did what all Irish people do on a wet afternoon, and stopped into a pub. In Chawke's lounge there were posters of hurling teams on the wall, there were silver trophies in a glass case, and a signed *sliothar* or hurling ball in pride of place near the bar. On the lounge television the Irish team was running onto the field at Landsdowne Road. Six or seven men were sitting along the bar and amidst them a young woman and her three-year-old daughter. Deirdre, as always, made friends immediately, and as the game started and the first penalties went to the English, the two little girls played together running through the lounge. Nobody paid them any particular attention, and the pub became a kind of extended family room with the children playing and the adults focused tightly on the age-old struggle of Irish spirit and English strength. Within fifteen minutes we were down 6–0. The Dublin crowd had quieted, and the man on the high stool next to me turned to me and muttered something in an accent so thick I had at first no idea what he was saying. Not wanting to appear discourteous I muttered something back in a tone of agreement and involuntarily began what was to become a kind of running colloquy throughout the match, my neighbor loudly addressing his comments to me and I responding by guess, having no notion in the world of what he was saying.

"They're going to wear us down," said another character along the bar quite gloomily, touching downward the brim of his cap in some kind of ritual gesture and at once finding a half-dozen voices to agree with him.

"They'll bate us all right."

"Oh they will."

"There'll be no Triple Crown this year."

"Triple Crown? Cod!" rejoined the first man, flicking down the edge of his cap toward his eyes once more as England went farther ahead. Another English score and he would be unable to see anything.

Throughout this, the man at my right, lodged on his stool between me and Chris, kept turning toward me and speaking quite loudly at a speed beyond my ability to understand. Up until this moment, I had liked to think that as a Dubliner now living in Clare, Irish accents would never cause me difficulty. From Cork to Donegal, I thought I could understand them all—until now. As the Irish team began to flounder in the mud, the customers in the bar began to take turns pointing out to each other the ridiculous weaknesses of our players. One was not to be outdone by the next: a failed pass, a turned scrum, and a new voice would swiftly join the others. If Dunlea was bad a minute ago, wasn't Mullins worse, look at that, would you? Did you ever see anything like it? Ha, look now where it's got him, now you'll see, try for England, didn't I tell you?

Meanwhile, my friend on the high stool continued to address both Chris and me in a beautifully loud but completely baffling dialect. Every time he finished speaking he looked at me intently, as if to see the mystery of his words swim to a dozen meanings in my mind. And, of course, out of courtesy and in pub-companionship I muttered something back to him along the vague tone of what I thought he had said. We were talking about the match, that much I knew, but what exactly we were saying about it, I had no idea.

He was a well-dressed farming sort of man with a genial face and blue eyes. One of his hands when he raised it up to enforce some point looked a little thick and stiff, as if that morning it had been trod on or kicked by a troublesome animal. But otherwise he was an entirely unremarkable sort of fellow, and seemed not to notice or mind at all that I never once disagreed with whatever it was he was telling me. After all, I thought, we were sitting here in the pub for the company more than the drink, and it seemed to me this was just the kind of thing that happened in Irish pubs. Quite cheerfully then, I humored the moment. I began, as in a remembered scene out of *Great Expectations,* to nod energetically, and I ventured to initiate some of the conversation myself.

It wasn't until we were deep into the second half after an hour of completely uncomprehended dialogue, with Ireland now trailing 16–3, that the man at my other shoulder tapped my arm.

"You needn't worry yourself about talking too much to Dan," he said loudly. "Poor man's deaf as a stone."

Saturday evening, with rain lashing against the windows, we dined on lamb and turbot in the Maigue Restaurant of the Dunraven Arms. The service was perhaps the best we had ever come across in Ireland, and that, too, helped sustain the air of old-fashioned hospitality. A pamphlet about the hotel declared it the foxhunting center of Ireland. Bryan Murphy, the manager, was a member of the famous Galway Blazers and during the hunting season booked horses to suit visitors to the Dunraven Arms. So as we walked into the lounge and recognized again some of the people with the green cards we had seen earlier in the day, I said to Chris, surely hunting is in the air here.

I was wrong. These were not horse people, they had come here for the winter sport of greyhound coursing and the J.P. McManus Irish Cup, which was taking place not three miles down the road at Clounanna. By nine o'clock the lounge was full of them, and a kind of low excited hum that was all dogs and money rose over the room. The green cards and pens were out again and stories of the speed and skill of hounds at the coursing that afternoon left no place for talk of rugby.

Neither of us had ever been to a coursing meet, so we felt a little left out. There were men and women in the hotel that evening who came here every year from all corners of Ireland to let off their champion hounds across the grass after the £5,000 first prize. I could already see that for them it was a passion; for them, this quiet weekend on which we had chosen to come to Adare were the climactic days of the year. As the evening drew on, the talk of dogs, form, and going did not diminish. Sunday, the man next to me explained, was when it really started heating up, and by God, the competition was keen this year, so it was, didn't I think so? I did, I said, as we took our leave and went upstairs to bed.

Sunday morning the rain was still falling as we hurried

down the street to the old Trinitarian Abbey to hear Mass. This was a lovely place of bare gray stonework and high-roof timbers. A polished brass plaque on the church wall asked that we "Pray for the soul of Edwin Richard, 3rd Earl of Dunraven, who restored this ancient church which was attached to the priory of the Trinitarian order of this place. He died on the 6th October 1871, Fortified by all the Sacraments." The man's spirit was everywhere in this town, and at morning Mass in such a serene and well-kept place, I imagined him further "fortified" by those who still honored his name today. The history of the building went back to the thirteenth century, to Maurice Fitzgerald, second Baron of Offaly, and owner of Adare Manor and its vast estates. It was the only house in Ireland founded for the Trinitarian Order, whose main object was the ransoming and liberation of Christian captives during the wars of the Crusades. The window over the high altar showed a prisoner with the chains falling off his feet even as a nearby cleric held out the moneybag of his ransom. The monastery had been suppressed under the reign of Henry VIII when the community of fifty monks was put to death one cold morning in February of 1539. Today, exactly 450 years after that bloody day, this building echoed with prayers to God.

We decided: Deirdre should not see the coursing. How could we explain to her why the lovely little hare was being chased by dogs?

Traveling with a one-and-a-half-year-old means being especially alert to her every movement, and devoting some hours of every day exclusively to her, whether out walking or playing in the room (or up and down the hotel stairs). In this way, I thought, we come to know places in a different way, living in them more than looking at them. For when you spend an hour or two following your little daughter through a hotel lobby or up and down the main street of some sleepy country town, you see the place in a new light. Since Deirdre came to us in the early summer, just two months after her birth, and especially after her legal adoption, just a year ago, we have had the joy of being a family — but you can't take a toddler everywhere, we realized; even when its not unfair to others, it may not be fair to her. Chris, a bit squeamish at the prospect of seeing coursing, anyway, professed eagerness to view Adare from a different perspective, and was happy to stay with Deirdre.

Leaving the Dunraven Arms in the early afternoon, I went back alone to Clounanna. Earlier that morning I had gone through the village in the pouring rain to try and buy an umbrella. There were none to be found, and in the hour before lunch we had taken to the Peugeot for a quick drive down the road to seek one. The next village, I said, was sure to have one. But Croagh was closed when we got there. A few miles farther on in the rain, Rathkeale had no umbrellas, only those borne by a hundred people coming from Mass. Newcastle West was a serious-looking town on the map in the lobby of the Dunraven Arms, but when we rattled into it, with the skies opening over us, four different shopkeepers shook their heads and looked at me as if I were quite insane to seek such a thing as an umbrella on a Sunday. After an hour's driving, we returned to Adare with nothing to show for our jaunt but a puncture, just as a faint sun mockingly made its way out of the clouds.

Now rain was belting down again, and hatless, umbrella-less, I walked down a long narrow country road in my

Wellingtons following the cardboard signs that said "Coursing." After a mile the road became brown mud; there were cars parked up against the ditches on both sides; and men and women, heavily coated, hatted and booted, were making their way in a long procession ahead of me. Only a few, in the elegant, well-cut overcoats and low shoes of Limerick City, were stepping gingerly across the ankle-deep muck. There we all were, in the name of sport, walking through the rain on a Sunday afternoon to an open field puddled silver beneath a gray sky. Dogs were nowhere to be seen but were everywhere in the air. Every car seemed to bear the signs of them: greyhound stickers, cages, warnings—"Athlete-on-Board"—notices for derbys and meets in all corners of the country. As we all traipsed through the mud closer to the gates of admission—a gap between fields—there were open-backed cars set up as stalls. Here you could buy Dog Diet, Right Stuff, Speed Pup, tubs and jars and cans of specialty foods "to make your pup a racing athlete," leashes of Moroccan leather, collars, coats of wool, toweling or fur; and for the greyhound owner there were coursing videotapes, form books, magazines, dog histories, and every imaginable kind of mud and rain gear with a special offer, this meet, on—umbrellas!

Everyone held a green score card, and near the field itself were a dozen bookies chalking the odds on rain-streaked blackboards and calling figures and names over the heads of gamblers. Fivers, tenners, and twenties were being rapidly fisted over; I saw one man put down a £100 on Flashy Star, then look around him to see me watching before he hurried off into the crowd. Two large covered terraces in front of the field were already crammed with people and abuzz with a gathering excitement. There must have been a thousand people there, and almost as many women as men. I jammed myself in among them and looked knowledgeably out across the empty field. Nothing was happening that I could see. The man next to me, wearing mucked green Wellingtons, a cloth cap, and a blue raincoat, looked up from his green card.

"Who'd you fancy?" he said in sweet Cork tones, turning his blue eyes and purple jowls in my direction.

"Flashy Star," I said, half under my breath, as if sharing top secret information. The Corkman nodded wisely and took up his card once more.

Up the field on a muddied pinto came a steward at full gallop. He plashed up before us wearing a long raincoat, and on his breast were what seemed to be red and white emblems or kerchiefs. Then, way across from us, a lone, white-tailed hare ran up the field, but still nothing happened. Men over the far hedges stood up and waved their arms about, keeping it on a dead straight line up the course and out into the safety of the woods at the end. Then the loudspeakers crackled. "Good afternoon, ladies and gentlemen, and welcome to the first round of the Earl of Dunraven Stakes. Into the slips now are coming Slippy Lad and Banagher Boy. White collar, Slippy Lad."

Every head was turned to the slips, away down to the right, and the sight of the two hounds in their white and red collars being set for the first course of the afternoon. Then the hare was off, tearing its way up the field by itself under the scrutiny of a thousand spectators. It was fifty yards up the course before the dogs were released. At first I felt a wave of relief wash over me: The hounds would never catch it, for the hare seemed to belt over the grass at such speed that nothing could gain on it. Then, as the crowd murmur gathered to a kind of roar, I saw the unbelievable speed of the two greyhounds as they flew after the hare, closing on it with every second, barely seeming to touch the ground as the hare ahead of them splashed a mad trail toward the safety of the woods still forty yards ahead. Almost immediately I realized the hare was not going to make it. It was all instantaneous, momentary. Ten seconds and the greyhounds had caught up. There were jaws snapping; they were about to gulp the hare, I thought, in a single bloody bite. Then the hare turned. It turned so fast the dogs went spinning, careening over on themselves, splashing, sliding over on their backs, and losing the hare as it charged off in a new direction. It took a moment before the dogs righted themselves, then again they were tearing after the hare at unbelievable speed. It turned them again the moment before they caught it, frantically dodging a trail through the splattering puddles until it reached the field's end and the safety of the woods. A winner was announced over the loudspeaker and the green cards of all those around me were marked as another set of hounds were brought to the slips. I had hardly understood the subtleties and pointing system of the sport at all, and yet almost despite myself I felt the thrill of witnessing the sheer speed and grace of the hounds. I had had no idea of the beauty of a greyhound in flight. Now I remembered that this was, after all, a medieval sport, a thing of kings and warriors. The old Irish sixpence had a hound on one side of it. Cuchulainn, the name of our greatest mythic warrior, meant the Hound of Chulainn.

Now another course was on. Again the hare made its way at breakneck speed up the muddy field. Again the hounds came, hardly touching the ground, and again the hare turned them and they spun head over tails in the mud. This time, though, the hare charged away toward the grandstand. For a moment, the hounds, stunned and shaking water off their ears, stood where they had lost it, looking faintly sheepish and ridiculous. The hare, I was delighted to see, was going to make it to safety amidst the crowd. It was tired now, running slower, right across to where we were standing, when all of a sudden the crowd as one began to roar and shout and wave its arms, frightening the hare back onto the field. There were whistles and yelps and cries of every description, and within a moment the dogs heard them, saw the hare, and came running. The course was on again. There was blood in the air. The crowd roared and the hare raced off into the very teeth of the hounds. It saw them coming too late and in a new mad dash, scurried right, then left, zigzagging wildly, plashing through puddles as the dogs tore after it, jaws snapping inches from its tail. The hare had two more tricks, more turns, more frantic, lifesaving dodges, and then the white-collared greyhound had it in its mouth. A kind of murderous quiet fell over the crowd and they took up their green cards once more. As the greyhound owners came running the long way across the field, the two dogs teased and tore the body of the hare between them, ripping it like a rag. The steward on the pinto held aloft the white handkerchief and the loudspeaker crackled. "Winner, white collar, Terenure Boy. Coming into the slips now for the next course are . . ."

I didn't stay much longer. More than three-quarters of the hares at any coursing meet escape the hounds, and more often than not, the hare zigzags its way to freedom, probably unforgettably pulsating with the exhilaration of victory. The speed and majesty of the dogs is supposed to be the thing. Still, I had seen enough. I walked out past the bookies and the cars in the still falling rain as more and more people came from their Sunday dinner and made their way in past me along that mucked road on the trail of an afternoon's sport—medieval Ireland still exists!

Today was a rare spring-like day, and early this morning we took a ceremonious walk around the farm in honor of "the day that was in it," as they would say here. We brought Deirdre with us and strode gaily out in the Big Meadow, the 5.844-acre meadow behind the cottage that we have just purchased from my father. All told, we had agreed to buy the Big Meadow; the half-acre tiny meadow at the very back of the house; the half-acre craggy field we call the Grove, containing the spring well and the pumphouse and the septic tank; the haggard, the cabins, the cottage, and the quarter-of-an-acre garden in front. Our purchase does not include the Tumper fields or the Bog Meadow or any of the fields and meadows to the east of us. But in a sense we feel that they will always belong to us. Deirdre will run among the tall grasses and wildflowers in summer. We will still think of it as ours.

It was so mild a day, with a white sky and no rain, that we barely needed the jackets we wore. Deirdre insisted on walking alone and although I tried to convince her that she had to be careful of the cow pats in the field, she still shied away from my hand. We let her make her own way and watched as she repeatedly fell, her Wellies getting tripped up in the huge cowhoof-holes that pockmarked the meadow after winter. Then she held up her hand and waited for assistance. In this slow, careful and somewhat mucky way we walked the Big Meadow.

When we had reached midway, Niall shouted and pointed up into Lower Tumper where a colony of very large, cotton-tailed Irish hare were running a kind of defensive play. Their long, loping jumps crisscrossed up the field. Magically, they had appeared from behind a thicket of furze and bracken. The three of us stood watching the five hare. Long, erect ears poised to the sound of our pursuit; white cotton-ball tails punctuated their flight like bouncing clouds above the winter landscape. It was the hour before sunset and I wondered what we had interrupted; for surely they had been in conference there beneath the sheltering, nearly golden, furze bush. Kiltumper is highly populated with Irish hare judging from the number of tracks that weave in and out across our fields like country boreens. They are well-trodden testaments to the fact that the Kiltumper warren is vast and important. Swiftly, the hare disappeared over the stone wall that separates the two Tumper fields and fled into another copse of gorse and bramble in Upper Tumper, probably making their way into the Bog Meadow on the top of the hill.

This was not a game of hare and hounds, but I would have liked to follow them. Instead, we followed up the bit of a tractor path that crosses the lower hill field and leads into the bog. By this time Deirdre was tired of walking and was well ensconced in Niall's arms and voicing all the names she knew of the things about her: bird, cow, goat, gate, sky, poo-poo, Wellie. To her vocabulary was now added, "rabbit." She was thrilled and it was thrilling to watch her connect words and things.

We paused on Tumper's hidden grave and looked out across the fields and meadows of Kiltumper. Turf smoke rose from our chimney in the distance. Our cottage seemed snugly cushioned between the bank of naked, aging sycamore trees bordering the western limits of our haggard and haybarn and the tiny pine tree forest that shelters us (somewhat) from the brisk easterly winds.

We crossed the ridge of Upper Tumper and peered into the Bog Meadow. No sign of the hare. We then picked our way across to Melican's bounds, to Toberreendoney, the Blessed Well. Last May, the month of Mary, we had painted the shrine with white house paint rather than whitewashing it with lime again. We had wired off a square to protect the spring and shrine from Sean's cattle. And we had painted over the red enclosure that sheltered two statues with sky blue paint. Now we clambered over the untidy stone wall that divides Sean Melican's farm from ours and hopped down to the loose flags that border the well itself and stood beneath the sap-dripping evergreens which grow about the shrine dedicated to Kilmihil's hero, Sean Breen. We were disappointed to see that our labor was lost. A patchy and mottled green fuzz had grown over the once pristine white shrine of summer.

I promise myself that before this May ends we will repaint the shrine, this time with a hard-wearing high-gloss paint, and fix the wooden door that frames the statues' enclave and tidy up the flags and stone wall. I envision a garden of ferns and foxgloves and harebells. Already I am looking forward to summer.

We called to Max, who had followed us up the fields and sat, as cats do, investigating two holes in the ground.

"Could they be the entrances to the Kiltumper warren?" Niall asked.

"Or a badger's sett?" I had once seen a badger scram into the spinney of furze and whitethorn just before us.

"Or a fox's den?" Niall countered. "Look, Deirdre," said Niall, "a hole in the ground."

The cat was pawing at the bare loose earth about the hole. "Come on, Max, we're off," Niall urged. But Max was too busy keeping watch, so we left him, his pure black shiny body lying in wait in the winter grass, black against the pale yellowy gold, like paint from a tube of Naples yellow.

We walked down the hill to a chorus of "Max, Max." Deirdre kept calling back up the hill for the cat to follow us. As we walked we talked about what we would do with *our* field now. Would we keep the cows? They would be calving, if at all, late this time, maybe even mid-June. If the cows were sold, would the goat stay on her own? Would we get a horse? Or should the horse be a pony?

And the garden? I have been forming my plans all winter to sow a lawn in the place where the potatoes grew poorly so Deirdre could run about freely without trampling the flowers or vegetables. Last year Niall and his friend Fergus hacked away at the bramble and blasted Japanese knotweed that was smothering the climbing roses along the cabin walls. This year we hope to extend the flower border in front of the house and bring it down along the cabins, making a huge horseshoe-shape perennial border with a

wee bit of a garden within. A horseshoe for luck. And the
climbing roses that have been there for God knows how long
against the cabins will make an excellent backdrop for the
new border that should get light (when the sun shines) from
earliest morning. Room for more poppies?

Spring is not far off. I'm glad that we're here.

· Chapter Two ·

Conversations on a horse—A walk from Sandymount
Green into Viking Dublin—The Spirit of Jonathan
Swift on a Liffey-gray afternoon

Paddy and Gerry, two friends of ours from the village, came by one evening, on the *cuaird,* a visit. We were having tea in our kitchen, and I ventured a question about horses and their likely cost, for horses were on my mind. Chris's father, Joe, and his wife, Polly, had written that they would like to buy a family horse for the Kiltumper farm. They asked us to find out the prices and where reliable animals might be available so that when they came over for a week later in the spring a horse might be bought on the spot. As always, we started the search by inquiring amongst our neighbors and friends.

"The price of a horse in Ireland," said Paddy, "is X to the power of Y, if you get me, Niall. The figure, as the man says, could be in the upper hieroglyphics."

"Do you know anything about buying horses, Gerry?" I asked.

"Nothing, Niall," he said. "Ask me the price of a horse now and you might as well be asking me the price of that cat." Then, after a moment he asked me, to carry the topic along, "Were you ever at any horse fairs, Niall?"

"Just one, just to see it. I never went looking to buy a horse. I don't know the first thing about horses," I admitted.

"I see. Well, do you know it's pure impossible to get down the street with all the people that come to fairs? You couldn't shift them. They'd stand out in front of you worse than cattle, so they would."

"Do you get a chance to ride one, to try out a horse at these fairs?" Chris asked him.

"You'd get to run him up the street and back," Gerry told her. "But what to look for, like, I couldn't tell you." Paddy was equally modest.

I could just imagine us, selecting some tame-looking beast from where he stood near the street lamp, gazing most learnedly at his teeth for some obscure reason like a species of country horse dentist, taking the reins, and running him down the street through the crawling traffic—and then being run away with.

We had seen one horse fair in Kilrush. From early morning, animals were tied up along the street, centering about the square where men with blackthorn sticks and hazel wands and low hats stood around and stared inscrutably at passersby. It had a kind of Wild West air about it, a kind of showdown in town in which the real trick was not disclosing your hand or, especially, your money. By evening, the dung and straw, and the sorriest unsold horses you ever saw, were all that was left as the pubs filled with dealers and buyers, tinkers (now known as "Travellers") fisting pound notes onto the counter.

We decided to put off our search for a horse until the warmer weather. Meanwhile our next jaunt was to be a trip, by car, to Dublin.

We, Chris and I, had begun as a couple in Dublin — in Sandymount. Nine years ago, at all times of day and night, I would bicycle over to the little house off Claremont Road where Chris boarded in an attic room overlooking the cricket field. She was studying Irish literature at University College Dublin, where I was studying American literature. In the evenings we would walk down to Sandymount Green for fish and chips, passing the pedestal where a bronze bust of Yeats glared into the distance. He was born in Sandymount, a stone's throw from the Irish Sea, the full width of the country from those Sligo and Galway places that have become "Yeats Country." Yeats seemed to fit nicely into the quiet of the Green. And I remember that when Chris sat her examinations the question on Yeats concerned something we had talked about the night before, strolling on the Green.

Now, on a windy afternoon not long after the fiftieth anniversary of the poet's death, Chris, Deirdre, and I sat on a bench in Sandymount Green. In small circular beds crocuses and daffodils were in bloom. All Deirdre wanted to do was run through the empty Green and point excitedly at the massive green shapes of double-decker buses gliding slowly to their terminus. It was twelve o'clock. And it was cold. There was no one in the park. It all seemed so much smaller than my memory of it. The lovely old bookshop that had stood on the corner was a real estate office, the fish-and-chips shop seemed to have changed hands. It no longer had the vaguely seedy, fishy air I remembered. There were more cars on the road and a supermarket had opened. But other things were the same. Sandymount was still one of Dublin's many villages, one of those places that embraced the mood and grace of the countryside while lying not far from the city center. Down all the roads that led to the Green the red-brick fronts and vari-colored doors of the houses evinced a kind of warm, if fading, gentility. In Sandymount Green the mood was intimate. Everyone knew everyone else: As we watched, two men in felt hats and brown raincoats nodded to each other, passed by, and then took their separate walks to the sea.

We sat picnicking on cold sausage rolls and scalding tea until Deirdre discovered she could pull the heads off daffodils and throw them into the air.

Then we set off, walking from our own past into the past of Dublin itself, from Sandymount Green down Newgrove Avenue to the Irish Sea. The red-and-white rings of the Pigeon House chimneys loomed on the horizon. In the rising, fading spume of their smoke is one of the images of my childhood: the power station by the seaside, the big smoke. My father worked for the electricity company and this power station was less than a mile from my grand-parents' house. The combination of these two things had made this building a focal point in my earliest view of Dublin. There was something fascinating about the end-lessly gray smudge of smoke always rising above those chimneys. In the Dublin of the sixties and seventies in which I grew up, there were none of the great smokestacks, factories, and warehouses to match the city-idea that dominated my imagination, only the chimneys of the Pigeon House at Ringsend. Unlike everything else it had not become smaller than my memory of it.

Playing cowboys with my brother Paul in the little back garden of my grandparents' house, or running giddily along the miles of strand, I did not know that Ringsend had been the scene of so much of the city's history. Here, for centuries, ships had arrived bringing invaders, merchants, soldiers, planters, foot passengers, and tourists, each gazing beyond their ships' bows at the immense possibilities for plunder, profit, or pleasure at Dubhlinn, the place of the Black Pool.

We turned from the sea at Church Avenue, crossed Tritonville Road to Londonbridge Road, and walked down the row of low houses and smoking chimneys that on our map was marked by the word "Irishtown." A strange linguistic relic, I thought, in this era when all our towns are Irish. Though we live in Clare now, in Chris's grandfather's house, in a townland full of Breen ancestral ghosts and legends, Dublin's Irishtown is my heritage. Here, down Londonbridge Road, is where my mother lived, and a little farther along is Derrynane Gardens, my father's boyhood home, the last little house at the end of the road with two upstairs and two downstairs windows. This was the place where I first discovered the idea of the past. There, in envelopes and drawers, were the faded photographs of relations who had died. Butter was still kept cold inside the tiled hearth of the unlit parlor fireplace; there in a glass case were old iron toy battleships that were taken out for us to play with; there, too, Granda's bayonet from the time he was a soldier in World War I. On a cupboard shelf lay the ungainly foul-smelling black rubber gas mask with its great heavy nosepiece that I was allowed to bring to school to show my history teacher. The scents and sounds of that house were the scents and sounds of Dublin to me: smoke, as Granda went down on one great knee and lit the coal fire with rolled pieces of the *Irish Independent,* holding a double sheet of it across the fireplace to encourage the draft; the thick smell of stout and the clink of glasses as Granda poured some for my grandmother (Granda worked at that most Dublin of places—Guinness's Brewery up the Liffey—and in the triangular cupboard under the stairs were the black bottles of Irish porter); the static buzz from the old wireless radio; the sound of the bread van purring down the cul-de-sac in the dark smoky winter afternoons, the breadman knocking on the front door with the black-crusted Procea loaf for the tea.

Derrynane Gardens and all the small huddled houses of Ringsend didn't seem to have changed much in the twenty years since I'd played there. All the little hedges and box gardens and railing gates were still the same. There was still the same sense of Dublin pride in these old homes, their bright-colored doors, roller-blinds and lace curtains, their close homeyness and warmth—their eternally smoking, inextinguishable chimneys.

There is a center to the past of any place, a site from which all building and generation has sprung, a first footing on the riverbanks. As we drove along Haddington Road and the Grand Canal in mid-afternoon traffic, we were traveling the route of one of the city's ancient pageants known as

Riding the Franchises or "Fringes." On a midsummer's day in the early years of the seventeenth century, the Mayor of Dublin, his council, sheriffs, and men took to their horses and rode from the center of the city out around the wilder fringes of the Mayor's jurisdiction, galloping out Dame Gate in a pageant of trumpets and banners. They rode into Ringsend and through the outlying and unruly village of Donnybrook, to remind the populace that although they lived on the fringes of the city they were not beyond its law. As our car crossed the canal and took us from the suburbs into Dublin, we were riding the Fringes.

The slow waters of the canal beneath Lesson Street Bridge were edged here and there with litter. It looked a sorry and drab waterway on a blowy afternoon. These were not the "Leafy-with-love banks" pouring redemption that the poet Patrick Kavanagh wrote about thirty years earlier; this water was not "stilly, greeny, at the heart of summer," but cold and gray and murky. There was a grubby, ramshackle air along the streets, as if the face of the city itself was smudged with newsprint, grayed beneath a wintry sky. Chris read from the *Blue Guide to Ireland* as we drove around St. Stephen's Green which informed us that there are thirteen avenues off this Green, one more than radiates from L'Etoile, as Dubliners like to point out.

I knew the hundred literary and historical resonances of the places we were passing. I knew that George Bernard Shaw, James Joyce, W. B. Yeats, Oscar Wilde, Sean O'Casey, and J. M. Synge had all walked through this Green. There were passages in half a dozen Irish novels attesting to it; Stephen Dedalus had thought "crossing Stephens, that is, my green," and that line was now written beneath a bespectacled bust of Joyce inside the railings of this eighteenth-century formal park with its lake, which George Moore had said was looped like a piece of calligraphy. There had been many Dublins in a thousand years, and the Georgian architecture and green parks of Merrion and Fitzwilliam squares, the perfect box of elegant Stephen's Green, bespoke the age of horse-drawn coaches, literary soirées, and civilized conversation when Dublin aspired to rival London as the finest city of the kingdom. To walk through this part of Dublin even today is to feel something of Dublin's claim to an elegance that is far removed from smoky pubs, tall stories, and pints of Guinness. But this was not the heart of Dublin for which we were looking.

Deirdre was asleep in the warmth of the backseat as we parked the car on Castle Street, a hundred yards from Dublin Castle and the commemorative notice of the gunshots and the dead of the Easter Rising of 1916. For a few moments we sat in the car and let her sleep. The street was narrow and empty and vaguely derelict. "T.H. Barnwell, Repairer," said the faded sign on the falling shopfront across from us. Next to it was a dirty red-brick edifice with the name "Bristol Buildings, Rebuilt 1897" cut out in the stone. How many times had something else been rebuilt and rebuilt on that same site before? Ten, twenty, a hundred? We had come now to the oldest part of Dublin City. In the square mile that rose from the south bank of the Liffey up to St. Patrick's Cathedral and through the Liberties, was the old Viking settlement of Dublin.

Deirdre awoke, refreshed and ready. We wrapped her in a wool blanket, strapped her into the buggy, and wheeled her out into windy Christchurch Place. Traffic crossing the city whirred around the bend of High Street and passed down Winetavern Street to the Liffey. Litter blew along the uneven path as Chris pushed Deirdre along High Street to our first stop, the ancient church of St. Audeon's. The streets with their cramped shops and bargain-price placards showed no consciousness of being neighbors of one of the city's most famous landmarks. At St. Audeon's was the last remnant of the ancient city wall of Dublin.

We reached the great wooden door of the church—and found it locked. We walked back toward Christchurch. The view northward across the river was marked with green-capped public buildings rising splendidly above the horizon of three-storied buildings. The green tops stood out all the more against a clear afternoon sky. When the eighteenth-century planners laid out Dublin's public buildings, it was decided that they should all be capped in green as a kind of remembrance of the countryside nearby. Since coming from the sea at Ringsend earlier in the day, we had constantly been conscious of the green humps of the Dublin Mountains on the south horizon. Their lower slopes were now shot with the white flecks of housing estates as Dublin sprawled ever farther from the river, but they were still there, the touch of the country over the shoulder of so many views of the city.

We arrived at Christchurch Cathedral to discover it, too, was closed. I shrugged my shoulders. Then the realization hit Chris; "Monday! It's *Monday,* Niall."

"Everything's closed?"

"That's right."

"I think maybe we've been living in the country too long," I joked. Deirdre looked up at us, wondering at the delay. "Well, let's just walk around here anyway."

We circled the railings, with the traffic rushing past us, before recrossing High Street and turning up Werburgh

Street to Dublin's other cathedral, St. Patrick's, and the famous heart of Dublin called the Liberties. The Liberties were areas once immune from city jurisdiction in civil matters, operating instead like little manors. Going down Merchants Quay, Winetavern, or Fishamble streets, we trod that afternoon the oldest streets of the city. A wooden church was first built on the site of Christchurch in 1038. Off High Street was a medieval craft center of bronzesmiths, tanners, weavers, blacksmiths, carpenters, and cobblers. Here, great hordes of chisels, punches, awls, tongs, knives, shears, and combs have been found—two hundred combs made of the bone of the red deer's antler have been found in Winetavern Street alone. These were, it seemed, not so much a refutation of the accepted image of unruly Viking hair, but a confirmation of the belief that Dubliners paid tribute to the Archbishop with the gift of delicate or ornate combs complete in their own specially designed comb bags, or caskets.

Now this area was one of the poorest parts of the city. No craftsmen's shops remained. A derelict and gloomy air hung over the streets as we walked Deirdre up by Golden Lane where a low stone monument on the corner commemorated the birthplace of the composer John Field, creator of the nocturne.

We crossed the street into Bull Alley on the edge of the lovely green park of St. Patrick's. Deirdre sat up at the sight of the green space and a set of bright swings inside the railings.

Just down the road in Fishamble Street stood the Musick Room where on April 13, 1742, Handel's *Messiah* was performed for the first time. It was given, "for the relief of the prisoners in several Gaols and for the support of the Mercer's

Hospital." Admission was half a guinea, ladies were counseled not to wear their hoops, and gentlemen to leave their swords at home.

Yes, here was the heart of the past, a part of Dublin seldom visited by the thousands who come every year to buy in the shops in Grafton and O'Connell streets, to walk in the serene splendor of Trinity College, or to pass the evening in the Abbey Theatre. This was a world informed by the spirit of Vikings, merchants, beggars, Archbishops, poets, boxers, musicians, and one of the most famous Dubliners of all, the Dean of St. Patrick's, Jonathan Swift.

Swift was born in 1667 at number 7, Hoey's Court, between what is now Werburgh Street and Little Ship Street, not two hundred yards from the site of the magnificent cathedral of which he was to become Dean.

In the early part of the eighteenth century it was his striding figure, walking everywhere, refusing coaches and sedan chairs, and working out schemes for the relief of Dublin's poor that dominated the five and a half acres of narrow impoverished streets that were his Liberty. When the English parliament of 1699 placed restrictions on Irish imports, the wool and silk industries around St. Patrick's collapsed, and the Dean took up his pen on what may have been the first of today's yearly "Buy Irish" campaigns. In *A Proposal for the Universal Use of Irish Manufacture,* he took the opportunity to propose to the Archbishop that all clergy should be made to wear Dublin-made gowns of black cloth. "Burn everything from England but her coal," was his advice.

Like everywhere else this afternoon, the gates of St. Patrick's Cathedral were closed, as was, just around the corner, the white door of Marsh's Library, the oldest library in

Dublin, which holds Swift's death mask, his writing cabinet, and the table on which he wrote *Gulliver's Travels.*

We were disappointed at this, but as a chill was falling on the late afternoon air, we hurried thankfully back toward my parents' house in the suburbs of Dublin.

Since moving to Clare we had made the trip across the country to the capital infrequently. As I was growing up in Dublin the west of Ireland had always seemed a different country to me. Now, living in Clare, it was the capital that had become foreign. Perhaps it has always been so in Ireland; the invaders' bustle and clamor on the banks of the Liffey was a world apart from the hymns and prayers of monks living on remote peninsulas in the west.

Now, with Deirdre asleep in my old bedroom, sitting downstairs before a coal fire, my parents drinking weak "Dublin" tea while Chris and I let ours brew dark and strong as we like it in Clare, we talked about the way we lived in Kiltumper as if we were describing the way of life in a place a thousand miles away.

"I've been giving classes in poetry to Leaving Certificate students at the house," I said. "The other evening one of them arrived with a leg of lamb under his arm."

"A whole leg of lamb?" my mother exclaimed, looking over at my father.

"Yes. 'We've killed a sheep,' he'd said, coming in the back door and putting down the meat. 'My mother thought maybe you'd like it.'"

"Imagine that, in this day and age," my mother said.

Chris added, "After last year's exam results, the mother of one of the girls Niall was teaching brought us half a dozen fresh mackerel and a bottle of homemade wine!"

My mother joked, "Maybe we should be living down in Clare, Jack."

My father, like the Dubliner he is, said, "Didn't I tell you the farmers have all the money."

We talked on for a little while and ate yet another superb apple tart made by my mother. I asked my father if he had ever been to the top of Nelson's Pillar, the famous monument that had stood in the center of O'Connell Street until 1966, when it was blown up. True Dubliners, he said, never went up Nelson's Pillar. It was the country people up shopping that climbed the stairs to view one of the widest streets in Europe.

"You should get up early," my father counseled, "and go back to St. Patrick's and go inside first thing in the morning."

"I'll keep Deirdre with me," my mother offered. God bless grandmothers.

In the summer of 1930, H. V. Morton wrote that "Dublin in the early morning, with the sun shining, is a city the color of claret." It seemed an extraordinary and unlikely description. When I thought of Dublin I thought of tones of gray not red, Liffey-gray in late afternoon, O'Connell Street gray on a Saturday morning going with my mother to Clery's to buy gray pants for Confirmation. On the morning after our walkabout, just as the sun came up, we drove from Goatstown back into Dublin in heavy traffic. In the near standstill, only suited men on bicycles seemed to make any progress. It took almost an hour to travel the few miles that was once wild countryside outside the Fringes. While sitting in the car, inching forward into Dublin, I looked down a street of Georgian architecture lit by sun-slanted morning light. The red bricks in the sunshine glowed like fire, and immediately I thought: claret.

Fifteen minutes later we were driving along the Liffey quays, moving against the river once more.

I parked the car again in Castle Street. It was not yet nine o'clock and the city was slowly rumbling to work. The day was beginning in spring-like sunshine. We saw a man chaining his bicycle to the railings of Christchurch Cathedral. His name, he said, was John Moore of Meath Street. He was a man of about sixty in a worn, greenish coat, brown cap, and bicycle clips, and he added the place name to his own name as a matter of course. "I've been chaining it here this past ten year," he told us, waiting in his bicycle clips to cross the morning traffic. "Before that I just leant it there."

When we reached St. Patrick's the front door was still locked. We moved along the railings and saw a small arched door in what looked like the Dean's own private entrance way. We went down to it and knocked. After a moment a man in black cloth opened it and, without a word, gestured for us to step inside the massive darkness. It was almost as if we had been expected, and as the Canon paced away, leaving us there blinking in the dimness and gazing up at the colored light cast by the stained-glass windows, we felt a sense of having arrived. As he walked away from us the sound of his soft steps died away in the obscurity of the aisles. There was a minute, a lingering darkness in that massive place, then a click of switches, and the great cathedral began to emerge into the light. All was stone gray. There were brass and stone plaques everywhere along the walls. Monumental gray statues were suddenly lit up, and, standing there, we saw them as so many ghosts of stillness, witnesses to hundreds of years' passage. Across from us, the first one we came to was of Carolan, the blind harpist. It was inscribed, "The Last of the Irish Bards." A few steps away was another moment of history, a great black bell with gold-lettered words: "To the Glory of God and in Memory of the Coming of the Huguenots to Dublin, 1685."

We walked slowly down to the end of the main aisle, where a heavy timber door stood by itself. There was a large hole hewed out of it, and beneath it this explanation:

In 1492, two prominent families, the Ormonds and Kildares, were feuding. Besieged by Gerald Fitzgerald, the Earl of Kildare, James Butler, the Earl of Ormond took refuge in the chapter house of the cathedral. He and his men bolted themselves in, so beginning the siege of St. Patrick's.

The Earl of Kildare, however, realising that the feud was foolish, as both families worshipped the same God in the same church, called out to Sir James and "undertooke on his honor that he should receive no villaine." Wary of this, Ormond did not respond, so Kildare cut away a hole in the main door and then thrust his hand through it in a gesture of peace. Ormond took it and shook hands, and the siege was ended.

From this has originated the phrase "chancing one's arm," said the explanation, and, as I stood there touching the ancient wood of that door and remembering the phrase on my own lips, I believed it.

The sound of bolts unlocking turned us around as a middle-aged woman in a headscarf wheeled her bicycle down the main aisle. She smiled at us as she passed, walking the bicycle into a room off the side of the cathedral. The soft clicking of the wheels and rattle of the chain of that bicycle came and went and then we fully realized the immenseness of the silence around us. Not a sound from the city outside penetrated the walls. We looked the length of the great main aisle toward the choir stalls and the banners, stalls and hatchments of the Knights of St. Patrick, then walked slowly from the place where a great Celtic-crossed stone is set aside in a corner. (It was found on this site. It is believed to date from the fifth century and to be the stone of the well of St. Patrick himself.) The walls were festooned with the stuff of the past, there were plaques, monuments of all kinds: To the Fallen Irish of Burmah, South Africa, China; to the Duke of Schomberg who fell at the Battle of the Boyne, 1690; to Robert Boyle, chemist; to Samuel Lover, songwriter and novelist; and dozens more. In the North Transept was Swift's Pulpit, table and highbacked broad-bottomed black leather chair. We came away from it, around the extraordinary altar and the most powerful organ in Ireland, and walked down the side aisle to the center of the place: here, beneath the scarlet-roped-off rectangle of polished bronze floor, lay Swift and his love, Stella.

We were sitting beside Swift and Stella when we heard a faint excited rustling sound from somewhere behind us. There was a swishing like cloaks in the air. For a moment I imagined I was dreaming. Then, from the very back of the cathedral, a man's voice began to sing to God. We didn't turn around, and only heard the choral angelic voices of children joining in the hymn. The loveliest music welled into the holy ancient spaces of St. Patrick's on a Dublin morning, just as it had for centuries. These were the boys of

St. Patrick's Choir School, founded in 1432, still singing Matins here daily. With the hymn floating through the empty church, the boys in blue cassocks walked in perfect unison up the aisle. They took their places by the altar, opened their books, and sang once more. The woman on the bicycle had left; there was nobody but us to hear them. The boys finished, closed their books, and walked in procession down the main aisle once more, turning left at Swift's tomb to go across the road into the Choir School.

We got up and wandered through the Liberties in the mid-morning, ending up where John Moore's bicycle was still chained to the railings. We went on to view the tomb of Strongbow, leader of the Norman conquerors of Ireland, buried in the cathedral he had helped to build. We went down into the dead air of the crypt and saw the old stocks of Dublin and walked in the very places of the city's beginnings. St. Audeon's was open when we got there. We saw the last blackened traces of the original city walls and the eighth-century "Lucky Stone." It had been stolen in the twelfth century, refound by the Liffey's banks 120 years later, and was now locked onto the church wall. When I placed my hand upon it I knew I touched eleven hundred years of others' hands seeking good luck. But nothing else moved us like those moments in St. Patrick's, the ancient heart of Dublin.

· Chapter Three ·

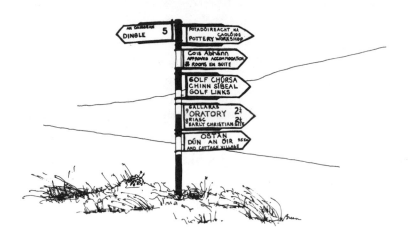

The Kingdom of Kerry—"Beware of Descending
Mist"—The View from the Dingle Peninsula—
Roads that were silver in the rain

Dingle sits precariously on the slim finger of its peninsula, between the mountains and the sea. Dingle, An Daingean, means fortress. It's a strange amalgam of shelter and danger with the brooding hulk of Mount Brandon at its back and its blue and red and green fishing boats nestling in the harbor.

On a blue day early in spring, Chris said, "Let's go to Dingle tomorrow." It was an expedition we had been planning to make and the time had come.

Some months after the first book of our adventures in Ireland was published, the phone in Kiltumper had rung with a long-distance call from New Jersey. The woman on the other end of the line had read *O Come Ye Back* and was considering moving to Ireland. What was our advice? I remember being hesitant and urging caution, while at the same time knowing the power of the Irish feeling and how a real love for place could overcome many drawbacks. A month later, Bonnie had called again from New Jersey: She was definitely going to do it. She had quit her job as general manager of a newspaper, put her house up for sale and was looking for property in the west of Ireland. For Chris, she had only one question: Should she bring her American Christmas-tree lights?

Six months later, a card arrived from Kerry. Bonnie had bought a bed-and-breakfast called Slea Head House at the end of the Dingle Peninsula and was open for business. Would we like to come down sometime?

It was April now, and indeed we would.

We took the car-ferry from Killimer and crossed the Shannon in such a continuous downpour that no one dared move out of his car. There were six in all, lined up on the open boat, sitting out the brief half-hour crossing of sea and rain that was our shortcut to the Kingdom County, (Kerry, Ciarrí in Irish, refers to King Ciar, a figure in the county's mythological past.) By the time the ferry shuddered into a mooring position on the south banks of the Shannon, I imagined the rain was letting up.

" 'The direct road southwest from Tarbert to Listowel is dull,' " Chris read from the Blue Guide. " 'Listowel, in Irish Lie, lee . . .' "

"Lios Tuathail," I leaned over to read.

"I really want to learn Irish," said Chris. She continued, " 'Lios Tuathail, the fort of King Tuathal, is a thriving country town but of little interest . . . Tralee, although the busy country town of Kerry, is devoid of any trace of antiquity. . . .'"

We chuckled, imagining Kerry outrage at such a description, for if any part of Ireland is famous for pride of place it is Kerry. Never mind. We both knew that Listowel was home to John B. Keane, one of the most popular writers in the country, and that during its Writers' Week festival it was a place unrivaled for talk, dance, and song. Tralee, of course, was the capital of the Kingdom, and the traces of antiquity there were not in monuments or towers but in the pert red faces, curly hair, and *glic* or "cute" eye of the people on the streets. There was a Kerry look, a Kerry air that seemed to me to be as old and real as the hills themselves. I remembered how, growing up in Dublin, it was the champion Gaelic footballers of County Kerry that had seemed to fist, solo, and pass the ball to each other with a kind of marvelous intuitive genius, moving up the field like a green and golden wave, glimmering like heroes in a boy's imagination.

Deirdre slept in the backseat as we drove through Tralee and saw the Slieve Mish Mountains looming coldly before us, brown and gray and purple, their peaks lost in rain-mist. We headed out the peninsula, with the sense of escaping down the Corca Dhuibhne way. We were going to a place that mattered for the beauty of the landscape and its heritage of the past.

Outside Tralee the houses became less frequent along the road, there was no traffic, and we drove on into the mountains rapt in quiet. The Conor Pass is one of the most celebrated scenic roads in all of Ireland. Chris and I had already driven its windy mountainous length a half dozen times, climbing its narrow curves into extraordinary breathtaking panoramas of mountainside and glen, rivers and stone. This time, said Chris, we'd go a new way, and taking a left turn off the road from Camp, she directed us on to "the scenic route" over the Baurtregaum Mountain. A sign warned that the road was unsuitable for heavy vehicles and horse caravans. Ten minutes later, the road narrowing and rising in a lonely gray ribbon ahead of us, there was another sign: "Beware of Descending Mist." We drove on, alerted, and a little giddy with the slight sense of danger. Water from the mountains had broken the surface of the road, and as we bumped our way slowly upward past the astonished gaze of red- or blue-bummed sheep, I realized nothing we met could pass us. With the car crawling at a steep angle into the sky, Deirdre awoke and began to exclaim. There were massive views of the desolate Kerry mountains rising and falling away from us as far as the eye could see. No birds flew. This is not a "scenic route," I thought; this is not a road in the twentieth century. We were traveling in a different time altogether now, for this was a track, a cart lane, a rugged wild windy pass through the mountains, a horse-and-rider route, an outlaw path off the main highways by which men with moonlight and rebellion in their eyes made their way unseen into the western reaches of Kerry.

Down out of the mountains the road ran to the right along the coastline of Dingle Bay. Within minutes we were driving in April sunshine by the three-mile-long silver-sheened sands of Inch beach, where a single man and his dog were walking one of the loveliest strands in Ireland.

We reached Dingle town by lunchtime, "one of the most

favored spots in Ireland for the independently minded visitor," as it says in Steve MacDonogh's excellent *Visitor's Guide to the Dingle Peninsula.* He's a local man and knows what he's talking about, for it was just that somewhat independent air that first struck me about Dingle. It's a place that knows it's different, that sits proudly on the edge of the west Kerry *Gaeltacht,* or Irish-speaking region, and between its fishermen and its pubs, flourishes a lively sense of Irish culture. There's Irish in the air here, and a special mood or Atlantic spirit that has attracted writers, painters, potters, weavers, and other craftspeople to make a life out here in Corca Dhuibhne. With Deirdre between us we walked down the hill of the softly curving main street, where the shops were packed snugly together and everything from woolen jumpers to seed potatoes and bicycle wheels was on display. At the Half Door restaurant we went in for lunch. Dingle is full of places to eat in the tourist season, but on a quiet Monday in early April a number were not yet open. As it turned out, even in high season, we couldn't have done better. The Half Door is a cozy, family-run restaurant and pub with a choice of fresh seafood and — that all-too-often-rarity in rural Irish towns — a babyseat. Sitting back after bowlfuls of absolutely delicious seafood chowder, plates of smoked salmon, and fresh brown bread, we made a few cautious inquiries about our destination.

"Tell me," said Chris, "do you know anything about Slea Head House?"

"Yes, out at Slea Head."

"Do you know the owner?"

"An American woman bought it. Very nice. She was in at one of our tourism meetings recently."

"And is it a nice place to stay?"

"It is, a lovely spot, out past Ventry. Just keep going. You can't miss it. Lovely, so it is."

Given that Bonnie, when she called from New Jersey a second time to specifically ask about the Christmas-tree lights, had in fact said that she had *thirty* trees to light, Chris felt compelled to ask: "She isn't a bit eccentric, is she?"

The owner of the Half Door hesitated, giving Chris a curious open-eyed look and probably wondering if she, herself, mightn't be the eccentric one, and then replied slowly, "No, not that I know of."

We laughed once we got outside. We walked Deirdre a little longer around Dingle town and then managed to persuade her back into the car for the last leg of our journey to the rocky end of the peninsula. The sun was out now, and our sense of arrival heightened with every mile as the road found the sea at Ventry and wound on between the rising shadow of Mount Eagle and the cliffside drop into the blue-green waters of the ocean below. Seabirds swooped and screamed in gusts, arcing up out of nowhere, gliding over the road momentarily and then sweeping off, holding in midair and plunging down out of sight to the sea. We had left the world behind now. Here there were no houses, no cars, no signs of anyone, only the sounds of the seabirds and the sea. Following the straight road I had a sense of things coming, literally, to a head. We turned a bend and I saw the Blasket Islands off the coast. They were the most westerly point of Ireland. I had never seen them before; for some odd reason I had never ventured farther than the town on my previous visit. I had only seen maps and pictures and the backside of the Irish twenty-punt note on which they floated like a school of whales. And yet I knew so much of their literary history. Like everyone else, when at secondary school in Ireland, I had compulsorily studied the Irish language, and read as a main text *Peig,* the autobiography of Peig Sayers, the story of her life at the turn of the century on Blascaod Mór, or the Great Blasket. It was not something I had warmed to then, seeing in its tales of the extraordinary hardships of island life, of drownings and sorrows, a kind of hopeless gloominess that seemed to overhang so much of learning the Irish language. What I had missed as a schoolboy was the true achievement of Peig's book: its feeling for place, for a life so closely bound to the salt-sprayed stones and rocky fields of an island that its words were pure expressions of the place itself. Since we had returned to live in Ireland I had rediscovered the Blaskets of the mind: the handful of books that had been written in Irish about the islands, which captured a world in words forever even as life on the Blaskets was on the very point of extinction. I knew now of *An tOileanach* (The Islandman) by Tomas O'Criomhthain, *Fiche Blian ag Fás* (Twenty Years A-Growing) by Muiris O'Suilleabhain, and other Blasket books, and had shared them with Chris. I knew that this was a unique place in Irish literature.

A gushing stream came down the mountain and ran five feet wide across the road falling through four stone arches in the wall to the sea below. We drove slowly across with a sense of entering. A mile farther on, white statues of Jesus and Mary built out of the cliffside gazed across the waters to the humps of the islands. A last bend and then there it was, Slea Head House, standing over the strand at Coumeenoole where the white froth of the water filled the arc of the shoreline and the Great Blasket lay directly in view.

It was a lovely spot, we told Bonnie, as she came to the

front door and then ushered us in welcome into the bright sitting room. Irish music played quietly on a cassette deck, and would continue softly in the air almost without end until we left. Within a moment, Deirdre was out of Chris's arms and staring down in amazement at a glass display case right in the middle of the sitting-room floor. Inside it were forty or fifty teddy bears, some in woolen jumpers, blazers, scarves, some hatted, some not, white ones, gray ones, brown and beige ones, and one with a tweed cap at a tilt over one roguish eye.

"That's not all of them, either," said Bonnie's mother, Margaret, coming from the kitchen, introducing herself and placing on the table a plateful of the first genuine American chocolate chip cookies we had ever seen in Ireland.

"Chocolate chips," said Chris.

"Docklet Bips," said Deirdre.

Bonnie and her mother laughed. "Whenever we have someone coming over from the States we ask them to bring us some chocolate chips so we can bake. Go on, have one."

It was like a giddy children's birthday party with the music playing, the chocolate chip cookies, and the teddy bears. There were clusters of bears and dolls all over the place, all brought from America and now at home in the nooks and crannies of Slea Head House, County Kerry. Deirdre had her arms filled and was walking around with two of the less precious bears clutched to her like old friends as we sat down for tea looking out at Great Blasket Island, listening to the story of two other Americans who had taken their lives in their hands and moved to Ireland.

Bonnie is a lively, blond woman in her late forties. Margaret, of indeterminate age, is kind and warm and supportive. Bonnie had come over and looked at properties all over Kerry, not for a summer cottage or a weekend place, but for her home in Ireland. Then she learned that Slea Head House was for sale. Once she saw it, she said, saw the location . . .

"Well, I mean it is the most beautiful place in the world, isn't it?" She gestured to where the waves were crashing into Dunmore Head and the seabirds gliding the middle distance. She didn't need an answer.

"Do you find it lonely? Do you miss New Jersey?"

"No," she said, with a little smile. "I honestly don't." Then, after a pause, "I've got great neighbors."

"Are they Irish-speakers?" I asked.

"Yes, they are," said Bonnie. "I'm trying to learn Irish. I've been taking classes since we got here, but it's an impossible language to learn. Really, it's so difficult, and even when you have some idea of how to spell something, half the time the pronunciation is completely different. And then two people might pronounce the one word entirely differently, then what with your *sheimhú* and your *modh coinníolach* . . ."

She sounded the Irish words with a beautiful west Kerry accent. I was staggered a little both at the strangeness of hearing the Irish from a woman from New Jersey and at the marvelous appropriateness of the language to the place.

Upstairs, Bonnie walked us along a corridor of small, lovely rooms whose simplicity I thought perfect. There were sea views from each of them, and nothing else mattered.

Unhappily there was no sign of the cot we had written to say we would need for Deirdre. When Chris mentioned this to Bonnie, she pulled a "cot" out of one of the cupboards.

"There's the cot," she said.

It was a fold-out bed.

"Whoops," said Chris, "that's a cot all right, but it's not an *Irish* cot." What we needed was something with high wooden sides, what they call a crib in America.

"So that's why Kathleen looked surprised when I said I had a cot," said Bonnie. "She offered me hers, you see, but I said I had one. I'll just go next door to her." Just as in Kiltumper, the problem was solved with the help of a neighbor.

Half an hour later, Kathleen's cot (or crib) had been set up in a room for Deirdre, and later that evening she climbed into it with one of her new teddy bear friends.

Chris and I sat downstairs in the sea-view room with Irish music playing, where Bonnie had started a little library of the Blasket books. She and Margaret joined us and we passed the evening hearing stories of their first days in Kerry and watching the fine light of the spring evening traveling between the islands. It was a marvelous room for sea gazing. A line of sunlight would angle through cloud and Inis na Bró would be lit, glittering silver, its strange stone skyline like some ancient Gothic cathedral marooned in mid-ocean. Another moment and the light would darken and then the Blasket Islands looked brooding in their isolation, cold and unforgiving, set apart in the western sea. Later that night, the moon slipped from behind the clouds and from our bedroom window our last view of the day was of those still, serene island mounds set amidst the moonlit waves.

In the morning a fine rain was falling. After a delicious traditional Irish breakfast of porridge, rashers, eggs, sausages, tomato, brown bread, tea, and toast, we wrapped

Deirdre from head to toe and set out to explore the end of the Dingle Peninsula.

The combination of such dramatic scenery — mountainsides sweeping down across narrow roads into thunderous waves, miles upon miles of desolate brown and green dotted only with sheep — with the great hush that lay over all of it added a timeless quality to its extraordinary history. At one time out here beyond Mount Brandon was the edge of the known world. It is 170 million years older than the Himalayas, formed of ancient rock. From Brandon Creek, Cúas an Bhodaigh, Saint Brendan is said to have set out for the "Heavenly Isles" and, traveling in a simple curragh boat, to have discovered America. It is a story every Irish schoolboy knows. What I didn't know was that the account of the voyage, the *Navigatio,* achieved great fame in medieval Europe and became a kind of classic adventure story full of danger, daring, magic, and mystery. This saga has been brought back to public attention in the last ten years with Tim Severin's excellent book, *The Brendan Voyage.* Driving through the rain on the road from Ballyferriter to Ballynana and on toward Ballycurrane, I could imagine what courage and faith it took for a man to set his boat into the water and be blown away into the unmapped world of the Atlantic Ocean.

We drove along on roads that were silver in the rain. At Gallarus Oratory, with Deirdre sleeping peacefully in the backseat, we walked up from the car to one of Ireland's most famous early Christian landmarks. The seventh-century dry stone building stands on one of the most scenic spots of the entire peninsula. As you walk up it looks like an upturned boat, its bottom pointed into the sky. Stepping inside and out of the rain, Chris noted how its perfect construction and design still kept out every drop of water. From the fifth to the eighth century a new way of life was lived out here on Dingle Peninsula. In Seamus Heaney's poem, "In Gallarus Oratory," he writes:

> You can still feel the community pack
> This place: it's like going into a turfstack
> A core of old dark walled up with stone
> A yard thick. When you're in it alone
> You might have dropped, a reduced creature
> To the heart of the globe . . .

The heart of the globe? Yes.

"People forget how important Ireland was in the early Christian world," Chris said. "Think of it, ten early monastic sites out here in about a four-mile triangle of land, and about sixty early Christian sites scattered around the peninsula." They thought they were on the edge of the world, and so they were. I could imagine it easily, imagine the hush of these dwellings out here at land's end; prayers and hymns tangling in the Atlantic breeze.

When Deirdre woke we drove to the ruined church and graveyard at Kilmalkedar. Beside the church was a building known as St. Brendan's House, although probably dating from much later. Into its roofless silence Deirdre clambered, touching stone walls where the rain ran down them. In her Wellies and a zip-up rainproof overall, she was delighted to be out, exploring these strange places.

"Kilmalkedar was a center of Christianity and scholarship," Chris read, as one by one we slipped through a narrow stile in the wall and into the graveyard. "A remarkable aspect of the churchyard is the survival there of pagan stones . . . elements of pagan religion were wholly suppressed but were continued in Christianized forms. The east window of the church is known as Cró na Sna thaide, or the Eye of the Needle. On Easter Sunday local people make nine clockwise circuits of the churchyard, keeping count by throwing pebbles on one particular grave, and some squeeze themselves through the window. Similar forms of *Turas* (rounds) exist in many parts of Ireland, though many have died out in the last hundred years."

I lifted Deirdre to the narrow Eye of the Needle; it was barely big enough for her. She stood there, at this ancient ruined center of Christian civilization, then a moment later climbed down to hurry out past standing stones, huge carved stone crosses, and gravestones that were marked: Seamus O'Connaire, Lost at Sea; Peadar O'Suilleabhain, Died in Chicago; and a host of names of the other dead. Sitting Deirdre in her buggy in the steadily drizzling rain, we wheeled away in silence down the old *botharin* known as The Saint's Road.

Back in the car, driving through rainlight and looking for a late lunch, we came to the Dún an Óir Hotel. It was not yet open for the season, and although Chris tried to fill the time with more history—the siege of Dún an Óir where Spanish ships had landed in September 1580 and where Sir Walter Raleigh and the poet Edmund Spenser oversaw the massacre of the Spaniards, and from which "Marú an Dúna ort!" (The massacre of the Dun upon you!) still survives as a curse—we were all becoming quite hungry. We were in the heart of the west Kerry Gaeltacht region now. All signs were in Irish as well as English, and there was not a car on the road. In the village of Ballyferriter we stopped at a pub with two petrol pumps outside. Getting out of the car to go inside, I told Chris I'd buy petrol and see if we could get some sandwiches.

"Ask in Irish," she said.

"No, I won't."

"I don't think it's right. Their first language is Irish and if you speak English you're forcing them to use it, too."

"I haven't talked with an Irish speaker in years," I said, adding lamely, "Besides, my Irish is so poor . . ."

"You're just afraid to . . ." She trailed off as a friendly looking woman in a blue jumper came out to the car. There was a moment's pause.

"Ten pounds, please," I said, and saw Chris frown.

"I wanted him to ask in Irish," Chris explained to the woman.

"Ach níl a lán gaelige agam," I said, a little awkwardly.

"Oh, we don't mind," smiled the woman pleasantly, and then to me, a word of praise: *go maith*.

"An bfhuil . . . eh . . . eh . . . sandwiches . . . ?"

She nodded yes, and a moment later Deirdre was freed from her babyseat and seated on a tall stool at the bar next to a fisherman from Dun Chaoin.

"Nice juice?" Deirdre asked him sweetly as he raised his glass of Guinness. He smiled at her and held out a finger. Were we visiting? Where were we staying? In Slea Head House? He was born near there. The words slipped from him in thickly accented English; they sounded foreign in his mouth. And when he spoke to the woman behind the bar who was busily buttering the sandwiches it was a strong gruff Irish he uttered, his mouth barely opening. As we sat there, the four of us, along the bar in the Ballyferriter pub,

Deirdre was the common language among us, and it was her antics, her giggles, her amazement at the froth lip left by the Guinness, her careful, surgical removal of each morsel of chicken from between the bread, that drew the fisherman's eye.

Not for the first time I felt a keen regret that my Irish wasn't better.

As we came outside to where the sky had cleared, Chris said, "I'm going to learn it through Deirdre."

We decided to take a walk through the village. Ballyferriter was empty in the afternoon light; it was a quiet, ordinary-looking village, but by midsummer there would be droves of Irish students here from all over the country, all trying to improve their accent (or *blas*), taking classes and going to ceilis, speaking good and bad Irish all over the place. As we walked out the end of the village and along the road toward Ferriter's Cove, I was thinking how aptly Irish words and sounds seemed to fit this place. You could almost hear them in the air. And yet I knew that among the current debates in Irish education was a movement to drop the obligation to study Irish in secondary school. German, Spanish, any other European language, it was argued, should be added to the French that was already on the curriculum. After all, in a country whose young were emigrating in great numbers every summer, what use was Irish?

Nowhere more than out here, at the end of the Dingle Peninsula, did such questions call forth sadness. The purity of the language spoken here had been almost legendary, and the green and rocky slopes of the Blasket Islands off the coast were a constant reminder of the men and women who had given the language some of its finest literature.

That evening, sitting once more in the warm comfort of Bonnie's front room at Slea Head House, it was impossible not to think of the lives of those writers, those who had lived out there across the rain in the now roofless shells of stone cottages on Blascaod Mór; those who had rowed fishing curraghs daily into Caladh an Oileáin, the island harbor; those who played games of hurling on the island strand, An Trá Bhan, or carried coffins to the boats down Botharin na Marbh, the Road of the Dead.

The rain had come in, veiling the islands, and in the deepening evening light they looked cold and gray. It was over thirty years since they had been inhabited, for emigration and death had gradually washed away the self-contained fishing community of the Blasket Islands. Once it had its own *Rí* or king, its own island folklore and customs, its own poets and musicians. Now, Charles Haughey, Taoiseach (Prime Minister) of Ireland, was the only official inhabitant of the Blaskets; he made his summer home in Inis Icileáin, preserving a presence out there on the westernmost edge of the country. In a story that seemed to capture some of the fierce spiritual attachment that people can form to a place, Bonnie told us how the local schoolmaster of the Dun Chaoin primary school had from time to time noticed people standing outside the school and gazing in. He had no idea what they were looking for or at. They came, often alone, gazed, said nothing, and went away again. Only later came the explanation: When the islands were abandoned due to hardship, the islanders' very beautiful statue of the Virgin Mary was taken across to the mainland by boat. It eventually found a home by the window of the main room in the Dun Chaoin primary school. Now, when sons, daughters, descendants, or relations of the islanders returned from Chicago or Sydney or the Bronx or wherever they were scattered, it was that statue they came to gaze upon through the window.

The last words belong to Tomas O'Criomhthain, an almost Homeric figure, who wrote his life's story on the Blaskets in *The Islandman,* and foresaw the end of island life. In the final pages of *The Islandman* he wrote:

I can remember being at my mother's breast. She would carry me up to the hill in a creel she had for bringing home the turf. When the creel was full of turf, she would go back with me under her arm. I remember being a boy; I remember being a young man; I remember the bloom of my vigour and my strength. I have known famine and plenty, fortune and ill-fortune in my life-days till today. They are great teachers for one that marks them well.

One day there will be none left in the Blasket of all I have mentioned in this book — and none to remember them. . . . Since the first fire was kindled in this island none has written of his life and the world. I am proud to set down my story and the story of my neighbors. This writing will tell how the islanders lived in the old days. My mother used to go carrying turf when I was eighteen years of age. She did it that I might go to school, for rarely did we get a chance of schooling. I hope in God that she and my father will inherit the Blessed Kingdom; and that I and every reader of this book after me will meet them in the Island of Paradise.

Mary Dooley Keane phoned when we returned home. "Crissie," she said breathlessly, "we were over today and took four bales." "Yes, Mary," I said, knowing somehow that this was not the point of her phone call. "Crissie," she said, "your hens are laying." She paused and I said, "Yes, Mary." "Crissie, they're laying in the bales!" "Oh," I said, "that's grand." "Yes, Crissie," she said. "I left three sods of turf on top of the place where they're laying." "Lovely, Mary, thanks very much." "Bye," she said.

I went directly out to the haybarn and sure enough, there beneath the tepee of turf set there by Mary to guide me were four lovely fresh cool eggs in the warm hay hollow. Delightful.

· Chapter Four ·

On the trail of the Cake Dance—Bunratty Folk
Park or, a sod of turf for the fire—Kilkenny,
Ireland's medieval city

Easter Week marked our fifth anniversary in Kiltumper. Chris's mother, also Christine, had come for a visit, and through her eyes we could see anew the shape our life had taken on here. We were a family now, and with the arrival of "Mom-Mom," as Deirdre called her, our cottage had an air of closeness and warmth. In the mornings Deirdre crossed the kitchen to go to "the shops" and returned with "the groceries" to Mom-Mom on the couch. Among the first things her gracious grandmother had done upon arriving in Kiltumper was to buy a gray carpet for the parlor-cum-studio and now, running from the bedroom, Deirdre madly circled on the new soft surface before coming into the kitchen.

"Oh lovey carpet," she sang and held Mom–Mom's hand.

As the preparations and prayers of Easter busied both the countryside and the village, I realized how much we took for granted now, how easily we knew and accepted the rhythms of this place. There were things going on here that had gone on for decades, and yet like anywhere else things were changing here, too.

In the evenings I was reading Kevin Danaher's book *The Year in Ireland,* a calendar of all the old customs and country traditions associated with the different times of year. For Eastertime he writes of the furious cleaning and scrubbing, the whitewashing and tidying that in every country house were a natural part of the preparation for Easter. In this way it was similar to Christmas, and in Kiltumper in Easter Week this year that same feeling of getting ready quickened the air. I felt it when I walked into Mary's house and saw her tidying out a cupboard onto the kitchen floor.

"Mary," I said, "you're getting ready for Easter."

"I am," she smiled, and sat down for a rest by the table.

After a moment I told her of the book I was reading and asked her if she had ever heard of some of the customs. "I know that on Good Friday people still fast," I said. "But did you ever hear that you aren't supposed to move house or begin any important enterprise on Good Friday? No blood was to be shed, no wood worked, no nail driven from noon until three?"

"I didn't, Niall, but people would be kind of quiet anyway on a Good Friday, you know. They wouldn't think of doing a lot of things, but just to be around the house and then go down to the church at three."

"And the sky was supposed to darken then."

"That's right, too; I've heard that, and sometimes it might be raining and that, and that'd be, well, you know, sort of respectful I suppose, Niall," she said.

"And eggs, Mary?"

"Eggs?"

"You know the idea was that on Pancake Tuesday at the beginning of Lent the woman of the house was supposed to use up all her eggs. And that during the four weeks of Lent she wouldn't use any eggs at all. Then, on Easter Sunday breakfast after Mass there'd be eggs for everyone."

"No, Niall, we'd often eat eggs instead of meat during Lent. But right enough, on Easter Sunday—there was no chocolate eggs that time—and my mother'd put down a good number of eggs and we'd all have plenty of them for the breakfast."

Fragments of all these traditions still existed during Easter Week in our parish. There was only one tradition I could find no trace of, and that was what Kevin Danaher called the Pruthóg or Cake Dance of Easter Sunday.

On Easter Sunday the cross-roads dance was held. A cake was baked—it might be a boxty cake, a griddle cake, or a barley or oaten bannock. A churn-dash was placed in a field, and the cake was placed on its top, and some flowers were placed on top again. There was no cloth placed on the cake as far as I recollect. All the "courting" couples of the neighborhood assembled, and each boy courted his girl. Then the dance started, and the girls shook their flounces and twirled their hoops, and the boys pounded the ground with their feet. When the bout of dancing was over, the best boy and girl dancer went out and took down the cake, and it was divided among all the dancers. It was regarded as a great privilege to have the dividing of the cake.

Although Mary, Breda, and our other neighbors all agreed that there used to be no dancing of any kind during Lent (the tradition of doing plays during that time partly grew out of this and Lent is still the season for our drama group), they had no memory of any "cake dance." But the following day, another of our great friends and neighbors, Pauline Downes, stopped by the house to meet Chris's mother. In an offhand way she mentioned that she had just finished baking her Simnel cake for Easter.

"Your what?" asked Chris's mother.

"My Simnel cake. I make it every year at Easter."

"Just at Easter."

"Yes."

"And what kind of cake is it, Pauline?" I asked.

"It's a kind of fruitcake with a layer of almond in it. Much onto a Christmas cake, only you put a layer of almond paste through the center of it. Did you never taste it?"

"No."

"Well, call in tomorrow then," said Pauline with a smile. "Simnel cake it's called."

Was this Simnel cake then related to the Easter cake dances? Perhaps; perhaps not. But the following day, sitting in the Downeses' living room with a thick wedge of rich delicious Simnel cake in my hand, I liked to think that here was some connection to the old tradition. Pauline's Easter cake was a solid reminder of the other aspect of the Pruthóg dance, for from the custom of awarding the best dancing couple the cake to be divided with the others had come a phrase still current in everyday speech here. It fell from the lips of ten-year-old Karol Downes without his thinking a moment.

"That's lovely, Pauline," I said.

"Oh," said Karol, "that takes the cake."

A cold rain fell. What to do with visitors, family visitors at that, on a dreary Saturday, a spring day that seemed like winter? Just sitting around drinking decaffeinated coffee, here in Ireland, seems a violation of the rules of hospitality. Since her arrival at the beginning of the week, my mother and I had chatted constantly. And Eileen and Phil Brown, my aunt and uncle, who had come over from London to collect an oil painting I was selling them, were in fairly close communication with us and knew all our news already. Only Lisa, their twenty-four-year-old daughter, was unfamiliar with Kiltumper. And although I knew that my mother was perfectly content to just be with us in our cottage home and play with Deirdre, I felt an obligation to show her some small part of Ireland. I suggested that we go to Bunratty Castle and Folk Park. So in the wind and rain, my mother, Lisa, Niall, Deirdre, and I set off for the Old Ground Hotel where we would meet Eileen and Phil for morning coffee before setting out for Bunratty.

Visitors to Ireland sometimes shy away from going to Bunratty Castle and Folk Park because it's labeled a "tourist attraction," and Americans, in particular, seem to think that this means *trap*. In actual fact, Bunratty is one of the finest examples of a fifteenth-century castle in Ireland. It was continuously inhabited until the nineteenth century and was restored by the late Lord Gort during the 1960s. Nearly every square inch of it is preserved and almost all the rooms are furnished with period pieces dating from the fourteenth to the seventeenth centuries. One of the nicest things about touring the castle is that one is able to roam and peer and generally investigate free from the constant roving eye of surveillance.

The rain did not let up. Niall and Phil had their Irish caps and wore them like shields against the wet. Deirdre, in her red, white, and blue rain jacket, seemed impervious to the weather. She followed behind Niall and Phil puddling through every little patch and pool of water in her path. My mother, Eileen, Lisa, and I huddled under the two flimsy umbrellas we brought with us but quickly abandoned when we entered the Great Hall of the castle.

Bunratty Castle has four square towers, North, South, East, and West, and each is accessible as long as one is game for maneuvering one's way up the four flights of narrow, circular stone stairs. I set out with Deirdre under my arm to tackle the South Solar Chamber, Niall and Phil and Lisa went off to investigate the North Solar and the private apartment of the Earl of Thomond and his family, and we left Eileen and my mother admiring the furnishings and wondering out loud, "How in the world did they ever keep it clean?"

The castle is complete with kitchen, bedrooms, guard-room, captain's quarters, and public chapel. It has spy holes and cubbyholes and secret places that appeal to the explorer in us all. And in the evenings in the Great Hall— the original banquet hall and audience chamber of the Earls of Thomond—it is possible to share in the reenact-ment of the medieval banquets of long ago, which, hosted by the Shannon Development Group, have a very lively reputation.

Leaving the shelter of the castle we once again braved the wet wind and headed toward the Folk Park and more hum-ble hearths. Bunratty Folk Park is unique in the Republic of Ireland, exhibiting exact replicas of rural and urban cottages and houses from many parts of Ireland as they appeared in the late nineteenth century. In fact, it was here that we had come four years ago when we were having trouble with our own two-hundred-year-old chimney. We found a cottage very like ours and sought out a man there who told us why our chimney probably wasn't drawing. If it had been filled in, as we told him ours had, to narrow the chimney's opening (allowing less of the elements to come down), then, for sure, the smoke wouldn't go up. "They knew what they were doing in those days," he said. "If they could have made it less wide, they would have. They were experts. No one knows how to build chimneys like that anymore." We agreed with him and took his advice, tore down the new flue pipe and cement and left it as it was meant to be, open to the universe. Thanks to the man at

Bunratty, we can now enjoy open fires without the room filling with turf smoke. We showed our visitors which of the cottages was just like ours.

There is the tiny, one-roomed blacksmith's forge, with smoky interior and earthen floor, and the North Kerry fisherman's house, and the mountain farmhouse, the Shannon farmhouse, and my favorite, the Golden Vale farmhouse, home of a wealthy farmer and his family, with beautiful furniture and artifacts and apple tarts baking in the kitchen. In each of the cottages that we entered a fire was burning on the floor of the open hearth and to each of these Lisa added a sod of turf. (Each night back at our home she went to sleep with the turf fire burning beside her bed in the kitchen.)

Apart from the collection of farmhouses, the Folk Park also has a tiny village. There is J.J. Corry's Pub, Sean O'Farrell's Drapery, Fitzpatrick's Hardware, and Cahill's Grocery. We were immediately lured by Brown's Pawnbroker's, where Phil bought a little trinket from his namesake's shop. There is a post office and a printwork shop and a potter's shop and all of them are open for business. During the summer months it is possible to see craftsmen at work outdoors, some weaving baskets, others operating the working corn mill, thatchers renewing the roofs of the many farmhouses that every few years need rethatching. But on this rainy, windy day there was no one about. We headed for the exit and to Durty Nellie's just outside the grounds of the castle for some hot pub grub.

There is a nice selection of gift items in the souvenir shop that is the final shop on the map of the Walk-Around Guide to Bunratty Castle and Folk Park. My mother was determined to buy Deirdre a pair of socks to exchange for the wet socks and shoes on her feet, but socks for children were not among the items on sale. Instead, she bought me a little matching jug and bowl of Nicholas Mosse pottery decorated with little pink pigs and green grass. I already had a blue and brown rabbit jug at home from the same collection and was happy to have the pigs, too.

Lunch at Durty Nellie's, which consisted of Shepherd's Pie for Niall and Phil and smoked salmon for the rest of us preceded by piping hot soup, was just the thing for a wintry spring day in Ireland. And we were able to dry Deirdre's socks and shoes on a hot radiator.

When we got back home, Niall and I decided that it was a worthwhile expedition and one we could do again the next time we had visitors.

"You know," Lisa said that night as she was putting a sod of turf on the fire and preparing for bed, "it might even be a fun thing to do on a sunny day!"

Our old friend Charlie had come from New York City for a week's visit in the first warm days of spring and, like any visitor to Kiltumper in fine weather, had been immediately thrust into helping out in the garden. For three days he joined us in the sunshine raking, leveling, and stone-picking the eastern side of the garden where Deirdre's lawn was to be laid. He wore gloves over hands more used to tennis rackets than pitchforks, and in an elegant white T-shirt banged the lumps of winter out of the Kiltumper soil. In three days the ground was ready. Deciding to let it settle for twenty-four hours before seeding, we packed into the car and set off for Kilkenny City. Charlie and Chris had been there before, but it was the only city in Ireland that I had never seen. Once again, my American wife and American friend had beaten me to it.

Only a few days before, Father Frank Feenan from New Jersey had knocked at our door, having read the first two books of our adventures in West Clare. Sitting back on the couch and sipping his tea, he had said, "Heaven for me would be driving a little car forever around Ireland, over the little hill roads, you know, and round the winding bends, just on and on, one county after the next, all the different green fields and the people's faces and so on forever." On our long, sun-dappled drive through the lush green valleys of Tipperary, I could picture him easily, puttering between those timeless places.

Going to Kilkenny for the first time was like going anywhere else for the second. For having read much of the city's history, its claim to being Ireland's medieval center and the most significant crafts town in the country, we were each filled with traveler's expectations. I had the feeling that I would somehow *recognize* the place I had never been. It seemed that the strongest image in both Charlie's and Chris's mind was the bridge over the river and the castle's reflection in it. (Of course, Charlie also remembered seeing a pretty girl there.) So half an hour after checking in at Lacken Guesthouse and Restaurant (where we had heard the food was the finest in Kilkenny), we had split up to walk around the city on this April afternoon and meet up later in the splendid grounds of Kilkenny Castle. Charlie wanted an hour or two to form his own opinions, to mingle in the city's streets and feel the humors of its people — maybe to see more pretty girls.

The sun was shining gloriously as we crossed the cheerful, clean rushing of the River Nore and walked up Kieran Street. Kilkenny is Ireland's only inland city, but the presence of the river pulses through it. You are always rising or falling, heading toward or away from the river. Richard Stanihurst, in his *Chronicles of England, Ireland and Scotland* of 1586, had written: "Kilkennie, the best uplandish towne, or as they terme it, the properest drie town in Ireland . . ." And in thinking of how a place might have deserved such a description, "the properest drie town" amid the mud and sewers of the sixteenth-century world, I recalled the feeling I already had of Kilkenny being particularly *civilized*. It was a feeling that would grow over the next twenty-four hours, but as yet all I knew was that we had certainly left the west of Ireland behind.

Up Kieran Street there were people coming and going in the ordinary bustle of a spring day. Running like an alley between the shops that backed off High Street and the River Nore, it was not the main street of the city. There was a sense of intimacy to it. A breeze was blowing, the air was light and buoyant, and the sun was warm where it angled down over the low rooftops. In all the best ways it felt more like a lane than a street, and yet walking along it I was caught by a vague sense of disappointment. It was a moment before I realized what nagged at me. I hadn't expected the informality of these streets, I told Chris. Imagining a place that bore the title "Ireland's Medieval City," I had foolishly and romantically expected more an open museum than a living city. I had anticipated a Kilkenny cool with an air of preservation, or a slightly exaggerated and self-conscious sense of its own antiquity. Instead, there was this marvelous essence, a medieval city within a modern Irish town. Between Kieran and High streets runs a series of old stone "slips" or passageways. There's Butter Slip and Mary's Lane, and narrow alleyways that rise through arches and round corners, moving you in and through the heart of the city in a way that predates all transport but foot and horse. The city forces you to walk, and no city seems so walkable. Down each slip and lane walked Chris with the excitement of an explorer. We separated and met up again, cutting in and out between the streets, walking lanes, and passages that had been in use since the days of the Normans.

At first we took hardly any notice of the fact that Kilkenny had been "restored" or "preserved," though we noted a general feeling of civic pride. Over the past five years, all the garish plastic shopfronts that have become so familiar in other modern Irish towns have here been replaced by more traditional, old-fashioned wooden fronts. No building rises above the others. At the corners the street names are signposted, the script neither too deliberately medieval nor too modern.

By the time we had walked the full triangle from Kieran to Parliament to High Street and out The Parade to Kilkenny Castle, the city had impressed its identity upon us. Kilkenny today still shapes itself much in the way it had been mapped out by the rich Norman settlers of the thirteenth century. Furthermore, a number of old stone buildings that had been fully restored throughout the city fit, side by side, on the modern streets. The polished limestone, known as Kilkenny marble, shines blackly and has won the city the appellation of the Marble City.

Here was an Ireland as far from Slea Head House and the wilds of Dingle Peninsula as it is possible to get. Jonathan Swift had come here to school, so had George Berkeley, after whom the California city and university are named. Kilkenny, we had been taught at school, was the site of the declaration of the infamous Statutes of 1366. By that time, this uplandish town had become an affluent trading and commercial center. It was a bustling place, alive with merchants and artisans, its street slips busy with buyers and sellers. It was said of the Normans at this time that they had become "more Irish than the Irish themselves," adopting Irish customs and language, and living in harmony in the thriving city. When the English Crown was alerted to the increasing "Irishness" of the Anglo-Norman families, a series of laws were issued designed to segregate the Normans from the native Irish, banning (among other things) intermarriages, associating with the natives, and, of course, the use of the Irish language. For thirty years the Statutes created tremendous strife and dissension in the city; ultimately they failed entirely.

In the middle of the seventeenth century a Confederate Parliament was established in Kilkenny in an effort to restore the civil and religious rights of Catholics. It governed Ireland through six years of bitter religious wars before being dissolved in 1648, two years before the arrival of Oliver Cromwell. The shadow of Cromwell falls over many towns and villages in Ireland, yet nowhere as darkly as in Kilkenny. Here, the monstrous ravages of his army have not yet been forgotten. He attacked the cathedral, shattering the fabulous stained-glass windows and stabling his horses among the pews. He desecrated a site celebrated for prayer since the sixth century, confiscated the lands of

Catholic Kilkenny lords, and drove members of the unfortunate Confederacy to the bogs and rocks of Connaught in the west. Cromwell's troops, idling in the defeated city, are supposed to have invented a game of tying two cats together by their tails to see them claw each other to pieces—the legendary, quarrelsome Kilkenny cats.

Today it is easy to imagine a parliament of all Ireland meeting here. And easy, too, to glimpse a sense of the past in half a dozen fine buildings: There is the Tholsel, originally the tax building and the center of the medieval town; Shee's Alms House in Rose Inn Street, a Tudor almshouse built for the accommodation of the poor of Kilkenny that still stands with a kind of grim, stone-faced endurance, looking up The Parade to the battlements and towers of Kilkenny Castle; and the lovely Elizabethan facade of Rothe House on Parliament Street, with its stone arcading and proud exterior, today housing the Kilkenny Archeological Society's library and museum, inside which, among other things, is a purple fingerless glove in a glass case beneath which is a card bearing the words: "Mitten left behind by Parnell in the Victoria Hotel, Kilkenny 1890, Presented by Miss Twomey, Dublin." I could imagine Miss Twomey, Dublin, finding the mitten, taking it in her hand, slipping it in her bag, putting it away in a drawer, taking it out and touching history in a little private reenactment of Parnell's evening at the Victoria Hotel, 1890. The Mayor's address to Parnell is written out somewhere else:

Dear Sir, We, the Mayor, Aldermen and Burgesses of Kilkenny are Proud to avail ourselves of this opportunity to congratulate you upon the collapse of the Foul Conspiracy initiated by the Hereditary Enemies of the

Irish People for the purpose of impeding the progress of Our Rational Cause.

I could feel the heat of the meeting and see the purple mitten falling unheeded to the floor at the rise of men applauding an oration for Our Rational Cause. Such moments are easily imagined in Kilkenny.

The sun was still shining when we met up again with Charlie in the grounds of the castle.

"This is a great city," he said. "It's just small enough that you can walk around all of it and really get to know it. You know what I think of Kilkenny? I think of it as kind of Ireland's Avignon, with its strong sense of the past. And look at this." He waved his arm toward the rolling, grassy slopes of the castle grounds. "Have you ever seen a nicer park in Ireland? There's a lovely path around it. I'm going to come back jogging here before dinner."

"Jogging, Charlie?" I said, smiling. "You're going to go jogging around a Norman castle?"

"Sure," he said, "this is a great place to jog. These are castle grounds, but they're also a park for the people of the city."

He was right, of course. We toured the one wing of the castle that had already been restored, stood in the long picture gallery and learned that the last descendant of the Butlers, the castle family, was now aged ninety-four, living in Chicago, and unlikely, said the guide, to produce an heir. Then, a little dry-throated and tired with history, we walked in the sun by the rushing of the River Nore and ended up in Langton's Pub, Pub of the Year in Ireland, in 1986, 1987, and 1988. And since there are seventy pubs in Kilkenny for a population of eighteen thousand, there is real competition. It was a splendid place, an old pub with modern additions: rooms opening on more rooms, turf-fires, armchairs, stools, and an abundance of cozy corners in which to sample the very full pub menu. Kilkenny is the home of Smithwick's Brewery, believed to have originated in the thirteenth-century Franciscan Abbey on Parliament Street. The present brewery, on the same site, dates from 1710. In the interest of research, and so as not to offend the city's most traveled product, Charlie drank a pint of Kilkenny's ale and found it mellow and sweet.

We had only a few disappointments. The Kilkenny bookshop had disappeared without a trace from Kieran Street, and Charlie, an American abroad, searched the city in vain for an *International Herald Tribune*. At the famous Kilkenny Design Workshops across from the castle there were no longer the craft demonstrations that were once open to the public in the converted stables. They might be reopening in the future, we were told, but there were many potters, leather workers, artists, and other craftspeople working nearby, all of whom could be visited in their studios.

Kyteler's Inn, an impressive stone building dating from the thirteenth century, proved a little disappointing, too. We had heard the marvelous tale of the place before ever seeing it: Dame Alice Kyteler had lived there; she had married four times—each time to prominent businessmen—and had become a wealthy moneylender. Rumors had once abounded about her: she had poisoned her husbands; her house was a meeting place of witches and demons. In 1324 the Bishop of Ossory charged her with heresy and witchcraft, she was imprisoned and condemned to be burned at the stake with her maid, Petronella. In true witch-like manner, however, the night before she was to be burned she escaped to England—where, presumably, one more witch would not be noticed! Her maid was burned at the stake, but Dame Alice was never seen in Kilkenny again.

There on Kieran Street was Dame Alice's building, its exterior beautifully preserved. And inside was a fine, clean, busy, *modern* restaurant. The mysterious air of the story had beguiled us, and although Kyteler's Inn is a good eating place in Kilkenny City, the feeling of dread and oppression we had anticipated was not there. Probably just as well for our appetites, we concluded.

It was not until the following morning, taking a guided walking tour of the city from Shee's Almshouse up to the splendor of St. Canice's Cathedral, that we caught a glimpse of what we were looking for. Instead of entering the main-floor restaurant at Kyteler's Inn, we were taken downstairs into the original cellar. There, limestone arches and pillars rose dankly to the roof. It was a secret haunt down beneath the modern city's streets. At a point four feet high the limestone was turning to polished black marble. Before we climbed back into daylight I felt a little shiver of apprehension and thought suddenly of all the shoulders that had rubbed against those pillars in seven hundred years.

Dinner last night at Lacken House was delicious. Niall started with potato pancakes, Charlie with marinated salmon, and I had smoked beef and duck. We all had the leek and Cashel blue cheese soup, which had just the right hint of leek and blue cheese. Charlie and Niall had the grilled salmon trout with almonds and I had salmon wrapped in lettuce. And for dessert we each had something different and were not tempted to share: homemade ice cream, chocolate terrine with white chocolate sauce and strawberries, and rhubarb and ginger tart.

One of the nicest things about the evening was when Eugene McSweeney, apron off, came from the kitchen and with a flourish presented each of us with our main course. I thought it was a particularly nice touch and one that seemed to embody the hospitality that Eugene and his wife aimed for when they opened this intimate guest house a few years ago.

This morning we set out in search of Nicholas Mosse's Pottery Studio. It's in a place called Bennettsbridge, and in Kilkenny City there is a sign that says four and a half miles, this way. We set out that way, but, as with most places in Ireland, Bennettsbridge was not well signposted, and as we neared five miles outside Kilkenny, we began to wonder if we were on the right road at all. We spotted a man on the side of the road leisurely gazing into a field. He wore his jacket and cap and seemed to be about sixty.

"Excuse me," Charlie said in his Yank accent, "which way to Bennettsbridge? We're looking for the Nicholas Mosse pottery shop."

The gentleman eyed each of us in the car, quickly identifying us as tourists. He was immediately helpful.

"Nicholas Mosse," he said deliberately, resting his suited forearms on the window. "It's up ahead." We all looked up the road, seeing nothing in particular. "Up there on the right," he continued, "a little laneway off the main road. Go up the road there, and by the chestnuts by the river, the road goes right. It's before the bridge. Down at the mill. Not the parents' house, now. You see, there's a bit of a notice there that gives indication of the person you're looking for. It's up there." Charlie and I thanked him as Niall drove slowly forward, none of us certain whether we were miles or inches from the potter's. But sure enough, within two hundred yards, beside the river banked with horse chestnut trees, was the "bit of notice that gives indication": "Pottery." In fact, we were so close that our direction-giving gentleman need only have pointed to the exact spot, but then he would have missed out on the opportunity of sizing us up.

There are actually two separate places to see: the shop, museum, and seconds shop, which are open to visitors, and the factory, which requires an appointment to view. Elizabeth Mosse, a gentlewoman and Nicholas's mother, came from her house and greeted us, letting us into the shop where Nicholas Mosse pottery can be bought. She was full of chat and told us all about how the Mosse family were originally millers from way back. This was the family home; the shop is located in an old cow house and the tiny one-roomed museum is in the harness room. She is a collector of Irish things and in the yard there is a display of old water urns and quern stones and milling stones. Years ago she and her husband started acquiring spongeware and she took us into the museum to see her handsome collection. She explained that the spongeware designs that are now a feature of Nicholas's pottery stem from this family collection, much of it Irish.

Spongeware is a kind of decorated pottery that was used in the nineteenth and early twentieth centuries. One hundred years ago, in most Irish kitchens, mugs and bowls of spongeware would certainly have been found on pine dressers and tables. Generally, sea sponges were used in applying the color, but today every sort of applicator has been tried in order to attain the spontaneous yet intimate appeal found in Nicholas Mosse pottery. His motifs, based on old Irish and Scottish designs, feature farm animals and cottage flowers in pinks and greens, and blues and browns, on an oatmeal-color base. They have names like pig and piglets, hen in nest, creeping flowers, cockerel, bunch of flowers, cow, field flowers, blue pheasant, and brown rabbit. And their appeal is enormous. His market is worldwide and his work is particularly popular in America and Australia.

Much to my delight we discovered that Nicholas was also married to an American, and this, to my mind, accounts for the extremely professional and organized nature of the business. (No, I'm not biased, not at all!) The spongeware is totally hand-thrown, hand-turned, hand-slipped, hand-handled, hand-embossed, and hand-decorated, and as one of their brochures states, it is "lovingly handled 67 times during its creation. Our pots are Mosse produced not mass produced." They use earthenware clay from Ireland, the pottery is fired in kilns using home-generated electricity from the water of the River Nore, and local people are hired to work in the pottery factory. It's as good an example of an Irish success story as there is, and it's all happening just here by the River Nore.

We left Bennettsbridge feeling rather proud of Nicholas Mosse pottery as we admired our four little bowls on the backseat. With the promise of some day (soon, I hope) ordering a complete set of dinner and salad plates, more bowls, and mugs to grace the shelves of our own pine dresser, we set off back to Kiltumper.

Today was Chris's birthday and after four months I was at last able to get the gift Deirdre and I had been planning since January: a purple and white MBK mountain bike. Although a size smaller, it was identical to mine in every respect. When I wheeled it up to the back door and told Deirdre to knock, Chris came out full-knowing what was going to be there.

"Mommy's bike," Deirdre repeated over and over as Chris swung her leg tentatively over it and pedaled in low gear around the car and over by the haybarn and back. In the fine April evening there was nothing for it but a family spin. So, with Deirdre in her seat at my back and Chris testing her gears on every slope and incline, we set off down the narrow bumpy road of Kiltumper. Our first true mile together in a way, for now smoothly switching gears and pedaling easily, Chris cycled alongside me at the same pace. As we passed Mary's house a cluster of the Downeses' children came running to the roadside to watch us go by and from behind me Deirdre giggled and risked raising a hand to wave. Then down the hill across the trickle of the Kiltumper River, up the hill and out onto the roads of the parish. Chris smiled across at me. She cycled level with Deirdre and pointed out for her the cows, the flowers, the stone walls, and in the distance the little plume of smoke from our chimney. A first mile, how many more lay ahead of us?

· Chapter Five ·

*"Road-housing"—A riding lesson—"I was looking for a
horse fair" in County Mayo—Knock Shrine—
A search for Moore Hall*

Ag bothantiocht is an Irish verb in which my ear found the
sounds, *bothar,* meaning road; *bothan,* meaning hut; and *tí,*
part of *teach,* meaning house. So, from *ag bothantiocht* I made
"road-housing," the true verb for travel in Ireland.

Today, with Chris busily painting, I took Deirdre's hand
in mine and set off down the Kiltumper road *ag bothantiocht.*
It had been sunny now for a week. Down in the village,
Frank Saunders daily consulted his "glass" inside the shop
door and daily warned me the weather was still unsettled.
Yet the sun shone. The countryside was gladdened with it.

Red-faced men in white shirts cycled to their bogs for the day, bringing sandwiches and tea. Children went pink-nosed to school, while their mothers, with beetroot-colored shoulders, left the house for the day to stoop in the sunshine and foot the turf. The grass shot up and the furze blazoned yellow across every hillside, while cows, out on grass after the long winter, lay blacker-than-black among the butter-cups and the daisies. Heaven in Ireland is a May walk down the sun-sheened road with my daughter's hand in mine, her eyes widening and her voice crying out in delight at the coming and going call of an unseen cuckoo.

We went slowly across the little bridge, out the end of the Kiltumper Road, up and around into Upper Kiltumper, across another little bridge in past Buachaill's where the garden had been set with cabbages and potatoes, and on into Dooley's. Breda was standing in the open door as I un-latched the farmyard gate. Two greyhounds were trotting on the grass before the house. We went inside for talk, tea, scones, and tart at eleven o'clock on a sunny morning. I heard the news and told my own: The chimney that was not a chimney above our bathroom was starting to crumble. Was there any chance Michael could come take a look at it?

On then back around the road and across the bridges to where May Conway's head appeared from amid a mass of pink flowers in her garden. "Won't ye come in and have a cup of tea? Wouldn't you like a cup of tea, Deirdre?" "'Up of dee," my daughter cheerily echoed and we were up the path and in the house in a flash. "Isn't it terrible hot, Niall?" said May, a lovely, gentle woman of seventy with pink cheeks and kindly eyes, as she wet the tea.

Holding myself to only one cup, and marveling at De-irdre, politely downing her second in half an hour, we set off again homeward. By now, it seemed Deirdre had fully taken to this game of *bothantiocht,* of road-housing. For as we approached the little hill up to Mary's she hurried me along, pulling on my arm and leading me in the gate. Mary's front door was open, too. She saw us coming and when Deirdre raced up to her with the phrase "'Up of dee?" on her lips, Mary smiled and nodded and led us into the kitchen. "Now Deirdre, you came just as the kettle was boiled," she said, raising the teapot and scalding it before adding the tea. "Ye walked all the way up to Breda's? Well a walk on a hot day'd make you thirsty, wouldn't it, Deirdre? And hungry, too. Ye'll have a cut of fruit loaf? Ah do, go on."

Who could refuse? We spent an hour with Mary, an hour of the true spirit of travel in Ireland, of tea and talk, talk of turf and gardens, of weather and forecasts, of how two of our cows had calved the same day, of visitors from America, of the news from Mary's niece Maura in the Bronx. And of little Noel Downes, who, in the middle of preparation for his first communion, called on Mary every afternoon after school, and after he came home from his first confession, told her with a serious face, "I was completely dissolved."

My belly swishing with tea, my mind bubbling with words, I carried Deirdre home past the Downeses. Our road-housing was done for the day.

"Well," said Chris, standing back from her easel as we wobbled up the garden path, "did you have a nice long walk, Deirdre? You were gone almost three hours. You're back just in time for lunch."

"'Up of dee?" Deirdre ordered, with a grin.

I phoned Burke's Riding School in Newmarket-on-Fergus today to ask about riding lessons. We had no horse yet, but I thought it best to be ready, just in case. The man who answered the phone in a lilting Clare accent was most agreeable. When I said, "Is this Burke's Riding School?" he said, "Yes, it is." Full stop.

"It is?" I said, unconsciously adopting the usual Clare manner. "Oh, good. Could you tell me something about the horse riding lessons?"

"Yiss," he said, "what do ye want to know?" (In Irish speech, it seems to me, an answer only comes as a question.)

"I've taken a couple of lessons and I'd like to take some more."

"When do ye want to come?" This caught me by surprise as I still hadn't found out anything about it yet. But his manner was most pleasant and it occurred to me that he must have thought from my American accent that I was calling from Dromoland Castle, the luxury hotel just beyond the hills from Burke's.

"Well, I don't know yet. How much are they?"

"I'm not the boss, but I think they're six pounds." That seemed very reasonable to me so I pursued it.

"Do you give individual lessons or group lessons?" I

asked, thinking surely this question would elicit a definitive answer, a schedule, like one might find in an American catalog, detailing days, hours, levels of instruction, prices—with the whole so intricately dovetailed that a tabular form of presentation was needed to do it justice. Something like: on Tuesdays at four o'clock there's a beginner's class; on Wednesdays and Fridays at noon, advanced jumping; and so on, including deposits required and terms ad infinitum.

"Whatever ye want" was his reply.

"Okay, so, I just say when I want to come, is that it?"

"Yiss, that's it. When do ye want to come?"

"Um, Saturday?"

"This Saturday, is it?"

"Yes," I said.

"No, this Saturday's out. There's a big meeting. How about Sunday?"

"Okay, Sunday."

"What time?" he said.

"Oh," I pondered, "one o'clock."

"Make it two," he said.

"Yes," I agreed, "two is fine." I had forgotten about the dinner hour. "Okay?"

"Yiss, see you then," he said and hung up.

And that was that.

Sunday came and I arrived at the appointed hour. I had no riding "gear" except for my black rubber Wellies, so I borrowed a hat and a "schtick," as they say in West Clare, for my riding crop. I met Kevin, one of the Burke brothers, a midsize man of about sixty in a worn tweed jacket, his sparse gray hair combed carefully across his head. He spoke in quick, breathy bursts of speech and I identified him as the same man I'd talked with on the telephone. The horse he brought out for me to ride was a chestnut-brown gelding, about fifteen hands high, named Vodka. Kevin gave me a leg up and led me on Vodka into the riding ring.

"Heels down. Very good," he said. "Now keep 'im going." With that Kevin centered himself on a barrel in the middle of the ring, keeping his head low and eyeing his hands. As I circled round him he occasionally lifted his head.

"Up down, up down," he said. "Up down kick." Round and round for an hour I rode, balancing myself upon the largest horse I had ever been on and posting up down to the horse's trot. Kevin stood and lit a cigarette, moving toward me and Vodka, and from his very motion the horse sensed a command and began to trot faster. I could imagine Kevin in his youth galloping across the flat fields of Newmarket-on-Fergus attired as he was now in his brown pants and hard shoes without a hat or crop or leather riding boots. Just a man on a horse.

No horse for Kiltumper had yet been found and we still had no idea just what a person might reasonably expect to pay for a small horse. Two days before Chris's father, Joe, and Polly, his wife, were to arrive, Chris spotted a notice in the *Clare Champion*. There was a horse and pony auction in Claremorris, County Mayo, the following Tuesday.

On a bright spring morning, the four of us (Deirdre would stay with friends in Kiltumper) with Polly driving the shiny rented Toyota, were about to set out from Kiltumper on a jaunt up to Mayo. I jumped out, moments before leaving, to call the Tourist Board just to confirm that the auction was on.

The lady from the Tourist Board gave me a pleasant hello. "I wonder, could you tell me is there a horse fair in Claremorris today?" I said.

She seemed stunned for a moment. "Just a minute, please." I waited; the others were still sitting in the car outside. "Hello, sir," she came back, "I'm afraid we have no information on a fair in Claremorris. We think there might be one in Ballina." Ballina, another hour's drive to the north coast of Mayo, and there only *might* be one. I went out, got into the car, and announced the news. She hadn't, after all, said there *wasn't* an auction in Claremorris, and besides, the jaunt to Mayo would do us no harm at all on such a lovely day.

The road went from Ennis to Galway, passing the left-hand branch of the justly celebrated pub-restaurant, Moran's on the Weir, in Clarinbridge. There's nowhere else quite like Moran's, nowhere like it for oysters in season, for mussels, smoked salmon, homemade chowder, or pints of the black stuff, supped down in the nooks and corners under the thatch and in front of the iron stove. While admitting nothing, this traveler can testify that a body, being unable to pass by, and presenting himself at Moran's for lunch at the unearthly hour of eleven o'clock in the morning, will draw only a quick smile from Mary behind the counter as she takes the order, hums to herself, and dutifully brings on the salmon.

Above Galway we took the road to Tuam. To our left lay all the brown and purple wonder of Connemara, the great lakes of Mask and Corrib, the Maamturk Mountains, and the great sweeping, desolate views of rock, hill, and water that have left visitors speechless with their beauty since time began. But we were not on the trail of scenery that day. We wanted the middle Mayo, the plain Ireland, the country town of Claremorris, which the Blue Guide dismissed as having no great interest but which for us held the promise of a horse on this Tuesday in April.

From Tuam on the road north to Ballinadine there was a Jack B. Yeats sky overhead, blue-striped through great bottom-heavy clouds of gray and purple, with the light yet breaking through. It was a Mayo-Sligo sky, there was a lift of light in it, a spring-like kind of buoyancy despite the threat of rain, its blue bluer than anything shining out of those marvelous early Connemara pictures by Yeats, brother of the now more famous W.B. There was a whole other feel to this inland Mayo; the landscape had an *ordinary* beauty, with nothing of the extravagance of the mountains and bays to the west. As we entered Claremorris town, I had the feeling we were in a plain man's, no-nonsense kind of place. I held my breath as we drove up into main street all on the lookout for horses.

There wasn't a single one.

At the end of town Polly stopped the car and Joe got out. We watched as he walked up to an old farmer in a green overcoat with suit trousers stuffed into his Wellies. He craned his head to Joe a little; some words were spoken, he craned his head some more, getting closer in on the accent, placing his ear upward to the tall American towering over him, and displaying the only black hairs on his head growing tuftily out of it. Joe asked him again, bending a little now to address the hairy ear and speaking the question down into it as if the words themselves were some kind of drops.

It was a typical, hopeless encounter full of good intentions, politeness, and misunderstanding, the kind of thing in which in Ireland a visitor can find himself involved for anything up to an hour, for within a few minutes, someone else is called in to help out, a sister Eileen, a neighbor, a shopkeeper, the question is asked anew and a whole series of new misunderstandings can begin—all spawned from the good-naturedness of the people and for the love of conversation. The quest for information went something like this:

"Excuse me, I was looking for a horse fair."

"A what?"

"A horse fair."

"A fair, is it?"

"Yes."

"There's no fair here."

"Yes, I see. Is there one anywhere near here?"

"There was talk of one all right, now you mention it. But it isn't here. There's no fair here."

"Do you know where it was supposed to be?"

"It wasn't supposed to be here, I know that. We haven't had a fair here in a long time. Sure there's no fair here, John?"

"No, Michael."

"No, you see. There isn't a lot of people buying horses nowadays, sure. They're mostly trouble, horses." A pause, an apparent cul-de-sac in the conversation, nobody moving and then: "Of course, there's a lot of 'em bought in Ballinasloe at the fair there, you know. That's out the year, September, October or that. That's a fine fair."

Again a short pause, a little pretend scratching in the ear, a touch to the cap, a puzzled, hopeless look that seems to look into the hopeless puzzlement of the universe itself.

"So there's nowhere else around where I could buy a horse?"

"What? Buy? I thought you wanted a fair. You don't have to buy at a fair, sure. Sure there's the horse and pony auctions on just down the road at the Equitation Center. You could buy there."

It was a mile out the road, a big corrugated green barn with forty or fifty lorries and cars with horse-boxes scattered haphazardly around it. As we got out of the car we could hear the muffled drone of a man's voice shouting numbers through a loudspeaker. Joe turned up his shirt collar and tilted his slightly battered tweed hat down to his eyebrows. Polly pulled her Wellies on, and the four of us walked slowly over out of the sunlight and into the barn.

It took a moment for our eyes to adjust, a moment of swirling dust in a beam of sunshine, then of horses, ponies, donkeys, and their owners moving in the dim, dusty interior beneath the booming of the auctioneer's voice. At a little raised table set out before three rows of benches he was taking bids from the floor as every class of animal was brought before him. As long as it stood, he'd sell it, I heard one man say, and didn't doubt it. I stayed close to Chris and watched as Joe and Polly ducked under a rope and disappeared among the animals and their owners.

"Well, everyone knows my father's here, don't they?" Chris whispered to me as we pretended to look at a poor unfortunate animal with a great dip in her back.

"WhatamIbidWhatamIbidDoIhearfivehundredFourfifty,forty . . ."

Certainly there wasn't a single person there who hadn't

noticed that we had come among them. No low cap or stern look could disguise us.

By the time five minutes or so had passed, Chris and I were both thinking the same thing: It was the people, not the horses, that were extraordinary here. It was like a scene from some silent film, all brown and sepia-toned with smoke and motes of dust flying across the light and a world of Irish faces captured in a country barn. Here were red-cheeked fat lads with Thomas Hardy sideburns and brilliant flecks of blue for eyes, there were bald-headed and capped men with bushed eyebrows and huge noses, others squint-eyed and small-mouthed, narrow-nosed little men with cigarette stubs always burning at the ends of their fingers. There were men of seventy and more, others impossible to age with browned, weathered faces and black eyes, sneer-lipped with sat-upon noses. There were under-cap eyeballers, slow smokers, chin rubbers, big men with small boots, small men with big sticks, winkers, blinkers, phlegm-ball spitters, and deep-chest coughers. They wore every description of cap and suit, of dusted or dunged trouser legs, old sweaters with colored darns, pants with stains on them, full suits with the seats and elbows shining. There were boys from school, horse-boys and young farmingmen, used to the life of animals and walking through the barn with muddied and worn Wellingtons like lords, thwacking the whinnying beast, settling her, moving her nonchalantly up to the ring. Everywhere you looked you saw another face more remarkable than the last, and I realized at once that this collection of men and three young girls had already established itself as a kind of tribe in my mind. For these were not just Mayo or Galway people; these were horsemen and women in a country where horses still possessed a certain honor, a place of respect and esteem. I suddenly understood why no one I had asked had wanted to help us buy the horse. Horse dealers, it seemed, were really a race apart. There was an air of secret knowledge about them there in that barn in Mayo, in which, however foolish, I imagined a sense of complicity between man and beast. The first lines of "Pegasus," Paddy Kavanagh's poem, ran through my head: "My soul was an old horse/ offered for sale in twenty fairs."

We did not buy a horse that day: It wasn't meant to be as simple as that, I told myself. Besides, riding an animal before bidding on it was not, it seemed, encouraged. And although Polly was an expert horsewoman in the States, even she was not tempted to gamble on a beast that had been tied up for the day in the dim brown light of the Claremorris Equitation Center. We weren't going to find the Kiltumper horse in Mayo, I said to Chris as we walked out into the sunlight. But at least now we had an idea of the price of an animal in Ireland. We had made a beginning, and came away from the green barn as if leaving another world behind.

"I only wish I dared take out my sketchbook," said Chris as we left. "What faces, what Irish faces."

I had never been to the shrine at Knock, County Mayo, although every year busloads of people from our parish and every other one in the west make the pilgrimage. The Downes family goes once a year. Mary Breen brought holy water back for me once. And a couple of times I have sent up my petition with a pound note. Today, being so close by at Claremorris, we stopped.

Knock has the full approval of the Catholic church and is recognized as one of the world's major Marian Shrines. It has become a very popular place since the last papal visit in 1979 honoring the shrine's centenary. A hundred and ten years ago on August 21, the Blessed Virgin Mary, St. Joseph, and St. John the Evangelist appeared at the south gable of the church here. Beside them was an altar with a cross and the figure of a lamb, around which, it is said, angels hovered. There were fifteen official witnesses to the apparition. They watched for two hours in the rain, reciting the rosary.

Outside the shrine is a great gray stone place with lots of space for people to gather in prayer. When we visited Knock there were very few pilgrims and tourists but tons of shops with row upon row of little plastic Marian bottles for the collection of holy water lining the windows. An overwhelming silence stilled us and made us respectful of the thousands who come here every year.

I was glad to say a prayer in front of the shrine, and while there I believed in the apparition. There is something unearthly about the enormous silence, as if God is listening. And even though a thriving commercial business of souvenir shops seems inappropriate, somehow the contradiction is forgivable. So, with the spirit on us, we bought two little Marian statue plastic bottles and collected holy water.

One for Mary Breen and one for us. And in honor of Grandma Kitty, who probably would have loved to have visited Knock on her only trip back to Ireland in 1971 when my father and I accompanied her "home," I bought a pair of blue rosary beads and asked forgiveness for not having brought her then.

In his best-selling historical novel, *The Year of the French,* Thomas Flanagan described Moore Hall as a wide, handsome house built with blocks of pale gray limestone, four stories high, facing Lough Carra. It was here the first Republic of Ireland, the short-lived Republic of Connaught, was proclaimed by French soldiers and Irish rebels in the summer of 1798.

Chris's father had enjoyed the novel and, since we were in Mayo, we wanted to see Moore Hall. We began the search, although we were not even certain if the place really existed. It might by now have crumbled to indistinguishable ruins, or have been pure invention in the first place. At first we drove on Joe's recollections of history: Wolfe Tone, Irish rebel and patriot, was in exile in Paris in 1798. For months he had petitioned the Directory to send a French army to Ireland to support the uprisings that had already taken place in Wexford and Ulster, and drive the English from the country forever. There had been endless delays. The risings of the United Irishmen had been ruthlessly put down and the revolutionary spirit gone off the boil. Then, at last, in a gesture more than an action, a force of a thousand men set sail for the west coast of Ireland under the leadership of General Humbert. They were to land and rally the native support, to gain a foothold, establish a garrison, and wait while a greater French army came to join them. On a summer's day in 1798 they sailed into Killala in North Mayo.

With a rabble of roused and angry natives armed with pikes and farm tools, the French army swept south through Ballina and Foxford on the road to a famous, if brief, victory at Castlebar. At Moore Hall, overlooking gentle, tree-shaded Lough Carra, the Republic of Connaught was proclaimed.

From Claremorris we took the road west past Hollymount to Ballinrobe. Lough Mask was before us, to the north Partree and Ballintobber.

"Ballintobber, I remember that," Joe said.

We turned right then, on the road to Ballintobber, past fields and stone walls older than the summer of 1798.

Chris had remembered that the famous early-twentieth-century Irish writer George Moore had come from Mayo and written a novel called *The Lake*. Was there a connection? Was this *that* Moore's lake that we glimpsed now on our right, losing it behind trees and hills when the road swung eastward? It was late afternoon. We were miles from Clare, and yet now no turning back seemed possible until we had found whatever stones were left standing of Moore Hall. It seemed a quintessentially Irish thing to do, to be rambling around a landscape that was no doubt littered with the stuff of centuries of history, now faded, disguised, hidden, yet still there all entangled with dream, imagination, and reality.

We passed historic Ballintobber Abbey. Here St. Patrick

was said to have baptized local peasants from a blessed well, and here now, on the site of the lovely thirteenth-century abbey, was the original starting point for pilgrimages up the mountain path to Croagh Patrick. Despite Henry VIII and Cromwell, Mass had been said in this building without interruption for over 750 years.

We moved slowly on around the empty roads by the edges of Lough Carra. Then, rising craggily into the sky-line, we saw it, the corner of Moore Hall, or what we thought was Moore Hall: blocks of pale gray limestone against a gray sky. We turned the car off the road and stopped before the two pillars and iron gates that led down to the house, or what remained of it. Inside the grounds, on the left, was a new low-sized bungalow with nobody home.

We walked around the ruins as if they were a monument, slipping through the bushes around the side to look out on to the lake. A scatter of birds rose off the waters and flew low into the reeds on the far side. The sound of their splashing traveled the width of the lake's silence, and again an incredible peace descended. The lake water rippled and lapped with soft sounds. The Mayo mountains in the distance were the color of old bruises, and heavy clouds of gray seemed moored in the pale sky.

Polly called down to us. She had found a way inside the building, and soon we were all climbing the cold curved stone steps to the roof. The floors had all long since fallen in, and now the stone stairways rose around a great emptiness. A hollow of history, four stories of exterior walls and stone stairs, and a drop fifty feet or more if you stepped into your imagining of any of the rooms. Gazing below us, it was easy to envision a little scene of nationalism in the summer of 1798, to picture men standing in the hall having come, victorious, from the field, an English army routed, balladeers and poets in the streets of Castlebar already singing the perennial song of the risen nation, and the proclamation of a Republic ringing in the sweet summer air that was blowing off the lake. We climbed to the last step and looked out through a stone arch. There, due west, across the treetops, was Croagh Patrick, the holy mountain of Mayo, with the pilgrims' road curving like a whitened weal on its back. It was a commanding, awe-inspiring sight. Lake, mountain, field: no man moved, no bird flew unseen or unheard. The wind stilled on the waters below and the smallest ripples broke in silence on the lake shore.

Later that evening, back in Kiltumper, we puzzled out the full tragic history of Moore Hall. Chris was right, Moore Hall was indeed the birthplace and ancestral home of George Moore, the novelist. But with the kind of twist that seems most characteristic of Irish history, the house, the setting for the declaration of the first Republic, was set on fire by a Mayo contingent of the IRA in 1923. During the civil war such attacks on the homes of old Anglo-Irish families were part of republican strategy. When a mansion was destroyed, its owner, it was believed, would move back to England, leaving the lands to be divided up among the poor tenant farmers. Added to this was the human wish for vengeance. Moore himself moved away, confiding to friends in Dublin that "Ireland is not a gentleman's country." In 1933 he died, and upon instructions, his ashes were rowed across Lough Carra to the tiny Castle Island and buried there beneath a cairn, a stone's throw out in the water from the ruins of his family's ancestral home.

Three days later, searching through the library in Kilrush, I found *The Lake,* a novel first published in 1905, about a priest's rebelling against his own celibacy. I read the opening page by the kitchen window on a May day in Kiltumper, and within moments was standing once more by the still rushy lakeside in Mayo:

> It was one of those enticing days at the beginning of May when white clouds are drawn about the earth like curtains. The lake lay like a mirror that somebody had breathed upon, the brown islands showing through the mist faintly, with grey shadows falling into the water, blurred at the edges . . .

Record-breaking temperatures these past few days. Twenty-five degrees Celsius! That's nearly ninety degrees Fahrenheit. Even thunder and lightning. This is unlike Ireland. It's almost like a hot New England summer.

Rain was promised for today but didn't fall. Rain is promised for tomorrow. I said to Niall yesterday, "We should try to sow a lawn every summer. Do you realize that it hasn't really rained since we first sowed the seed?"

Five summers and we've never before had weather like this. Warm sunshine has brought on the flowers. The garden looks spectacular. Less than ten days ago there wasn't a single poppy in bloom and now there are dozens. The lupins have blossomed in four days. Someone asked me the other day what I had growing in my garden. I started to name the plants of my cottage garden—phlox, columbine, roses, centurea, wallflowers, forget-me-nots, herbs, daisies, primulas, bulbs, dahlias, veronica, cerastium, arabis, campanula, delphinium—until I realized that I must have at least fifty different plants and a few I don't even know the names of. As they say, it's a growing obsession. The other day a woman who stopped by to admire the garden told me:

If you want to be happy for a day, get drunk.
If you want to be happy for a year, get married.
But, if you want to be happy for a lifetime, get gardening.

I think she may be right. There is always something to do, whether weeding, planting, or replanting, reclaiming, or building. In fact, there is so much to do that it sometimes seems as if there isn't any time left to simply enjoy it. Last year I built a little suntrap to catch the fading evening light before it disappears behind the aged sycamore trees. Those trees are well over a hundred years old. And at the end of a summer's day, I often sit out there catching the last warm rays of the sun and looking at the garden and planning my next project. I have many in mind. This year we have made a lawn for Deirdre to play on, and I have built a stone stile so that people can walk around to the front of the house from the back. We have stretched chicken wire over part of one of the stone cabins and have planted a clematis. The biggest success this year has definitely been the wildflower garden sown with native California wildflowers. Still on the drawing board is a garden walkway made of Moher flagstone and eight raised vegetable beds. Will we ever get the garden finished? I hope not . . .

We've been getting many unexpected visitors to our home lately. But we were eagerly looking forward to these particular guests. I'd said I'd "do" sandwiches and tea. We were expecting them around one.

Virginia and Ed McCaskey (or "Big Ed" as he is called by the supporters and members of the Chicago Bears) were traveling with Ed's brother Tom and his wife, Betty. It was a thrill for us to have them come to see us. Our Chicago Bears sideline-coach coats that Ed had sent us over a year ago after reading our first book, *O Come Ye Back*, hang just inside the kitchen door. They are incredibly warm. I wear mine often and can be seen around the village in winter in a great blue down coat that cradles me like a life preserver and floats me down the streets of Ennis like a great blue balloon. There's even room for Deirdre inside mine and her little head can be seen just below my chin.

The McCaskeys are two of our supporters. They cheer us on and admire what we have chosen to do with our lives. Virginia, the mother of eleven herself, was delighted to meet Deirdre, and I told her we were on the waiting list for another child. She asked to see my paintings. I was sorry to have nothing new to show, as I had been busy working on the "cover" painting of this book, *Bicycles on Gortnaheera*, which Niall wants to keep, and doing new pen-and-ink sketches. I am a very slow painter. She called Ed in and, together, they decided to buy the last two of what I call my Kiltumper still lifes: *Cowslip* for themselves, one

of my favorites, and *Jug with Fruit* for their friends, the
Rooneys of the Pittsburgh Steelers. Now I have no paintings left to sell but ample encouragement to paint more.

We said goodbye, and Ed's last words to us were, "Keep
the Bears in your prayers." I said I would. Right next to the
Giants.

· Chapter Six ·

*The Ceili Mor at Cois na Habna—Fleadh Nua in
Ennis, or dancing in the streets—The Hush of
Inisheer—Bicycling on an island*

It was eight o'clock on a Thursday morning. Ceili music
was playing on the radio, Chris and I, still clad in our
pajamas, were dancing, hop two three, around the kitchen.
Our heads jigging up and down, flashing past the window
and round again, we were mad Irish clockwork figures,
characters of the May morning spinning and wheeling and
housing away to the fiddles, pipes, and whistles of the Tulla
Ceili Band.

We were mad for dancing.

Every Thursday evening at nine o'clock for three months

of the winter we had gathered down at the school with four or five other couples to learn Irish folk dancing, "set dancing." Beside us were the Normoyles, the Reidys, the McMahons, the Cotters, and our great friends the Hartys. Our dancing master was Noel Conway. He taught us, with patience and bemusement, the Clare Set (also known as the Caledonian Set), in much the same way it has been taught and danced in the west of Ireland for a hundred years. Most of the Irish, particularly those reared in the west, have at one time or another danced a set. In country pubs or in wedding halls and in kitchens around the country, set dancing is still a great pastime.

The Clare Set is composed of six figures: three reels, followed by a jig, another reel, and a hornpipe. Four couples make up a set: They stand in a square and dance in a circle, and if that isn't confusing enough, one couple are "tops," another "tails," and the other two are both known as sides. In olden days, the tops were the couple standing at the kitchen dresser, and opposite them were the tails, standing with their backs to the hearth. The best dancer always won the place of honor at the hearth and when he rose from his seat to dance a set, the host would say to him, "You're for the flag." His dancing, drumming feet, then, kept time on the flagstone before the hearth. His "battering" could be heard throughout the house.

It is unclear from the annals of history when Irish folk dancing began. In fact, in eleventh-century, pre-Norman Ireland, when Irish was the only language, there doesn't appear to have been any word for dancing. The word *leimneach,* its primary meaning being leaping, was used to translate the Latin word *saltare,* to dance, in describing Salome's dance before Herod. But most historians discount the assumption that because no Irish word exists for the activity of dancing that the activity itself was unknown in ancient Ireland.

The Normans introduced "round" dancing in Ireland around the twelfth century, and later, dancing inside "The Pale" (the area in and around mid-sixteenth-century Dublin) was extremely tame in comparison to dancing done "beyond the Pale." The dance names themselves indicate what an exciting amusement was the folk dancing of the pre-Anglo-Irish countryside. "The sword dance," "A dance of ranks with change of music," and "The long dance with the sporting of young maidens" are just a few examples.

The word "ceili" in some parts of Ireland means a gathering of neighbors in the evening. In Clare this is known as "making a cuaird," or a visit; no musical entertainment or dancing is implied. So using the word "ceili" to describe organized dancing is, in fact, a misnomer, but the borrowing of the word is justified by the qualities of sociability and friendliness that are inherent in the ceilis of today.

Ironically, the first organized ceili was held on October 30, 1897, in London.

The long-awaited night of our own Ceili Mór had been Friday, January 27, at half past eight in Cois na Habhna, in Ennis. It was arranged that we would meet the other members of "our set" there, Brendan and Geraldine, Noel and Moira, and Liz and her nondancing husband, Aidan. Michael and Gerry were coming with us but at the last minute Gerry had to stay home with a sick child. That left Michael without his partner. But as the saying goes, "Is olc an gaoith na seadann le duine eigan," or "it's an ill wind that blows nobody good." Michael and Liz teamed up and the Kilmihil set was completed.

Cois na Habna is a wooden decagonal-shaped building ideally suited for ceilis. In keeping with the philosophy of Comhaltas Ceoltoiri na hEirinn, the organization of Irish traditional musicians and a body dedicated to the preservation of Irish music and dance, all functions held within Cois na Habna must be strictly involved with the traditional aspects of Irish culture. And on that night, the national chairman of Comhaltas Ceoltoiri na hEirinn, Labhrás O Murchú, came from Dublin to participate in the grand occasion of an evening's meal and a ceili dance.

Chris and I were very keyed-up for the night. We had practiced in our kitchen for hours, with little Deirdre sounding the steps with us, "hop two, three, and a two two three, and a three two three, and four two three . . ." We had danced down at the school with the rest of our set and we had danced over at the Hartys'. We had even shown Mary Breen, our neighbor, our steps one day out on the road when a group of us went walking one Sunday afternoon. She giggled and said, "Oh ye have it, Niall, so you do," and she danced part of a reel herself, lilting the tune and wheeling me around and around on a boreen in Kiltumper.

The air was filled with the quick lively sounds of fiddles. The Kilmihil set met over near the front doors while twenty-five or so other sets established themselves around the room. One of the band members announced that the first set would be a Clare Set and the dancing began. But were we ready? Was the Kilmihil set assembled? No, we weren't. There was a moment of panic when Noel shouted, "Where's my wife? Where is Moira?" But it was too late for a search party, the set had begun. We had rehearsed this so often that when the music began, the dance took over and our feet flew away to the rhythm of the reel. We were holding hands and advancing and retreating in the opening steps of the first figure. Chris and I and Brendan and Geraldine were declared tops and tails and in a flash, we were off halfway around the "house," and advancing and retreating. Fortunately, just then, Chris whispered to me the crucial reminder "own place," which meant that we were to dance a measure in our own place before another advance and retreat and halfway around the house to "their place" before coming home again.

In unison the room bellowed with the excited sounds of 250 people in shared activity. The tops and tails and the sides joined together in one loud burst of exuberance. It was as if we were all members of a team in a contest and our team was winning. All around the room, the tops, tails, and sides of each and every set advanced to the center of their squares and retreated. Smiles abounded.

I have to say that we were beside ourselves with joy. Pure joy.

Our classes in the Clare Set were over, but we were determined to keep up the dancing. The patterns and movements of the six figures of the dance—so many advances and retreats, dances in your own place, dances in their place, changes, houses, and halfs—were like masses of complex formulae, impossible to remember unless they were danced out, fleshed into the music. A month had passed since we had last danced a set at the drama group's end-of-season dinner at Sean Fitzpatrick's pub in Kilmihil, and, feeling the figures slipping away in memory, we flew into a panic at the realization of the weekend that was upon us: the Fleadh Nua (meaning the "new" *fleadh*) in Ennis.

Visitors often pronounce fleadh wrongly. It is fla as in *ha,* not flaid as in plaid. But they rightly believe it has something to do with the music issuing from pub to pub along the streets of the town. No matter how precisely the programs and posters announced the times and dates for concerts and ceilis, the fleadh itself existed beyond them. It was a condition more than a series of events, a state of music that took over the town for an official four or five days and often lingered on for days more at a time. It was the most Irish thing in the world. And yet it was also a formal attempt to put a shape on the informal nature of Irish music and musicians alike, which invariably resulted in a kind of giddy chaos of comedy, characters, jigs, and reels, known in Ireland collectively as *craic.*

The *Champion* announced details of the program: Official Opening with the Tulla Ceili Band; Lunchtime session with Sonny Murray on concertina; Dancing Workshop with Pat Liddy; Scoil Fleadh Nua with classes in Singing, Accordion, Timber Flute, Tin Whistle, Fiddle; Clanntrai; the family talent competition; dancing in O'Connell Square all day Saturday; Píob is Bodhran celebrity concert; Cultural Parade and open air sessions; and best of all, ceilis with the Tulla and Liverpool Ceili Bands. The theme of the Fleadh Nua this year in the bicentenary of the French Revolution was Ireland's links with France and, not least, the ill–fated fleet of General Humbert in the Year of the French. A number of French musicians would be joining the sessions, the cultural attaché of the French Embassy would be here, and the Sean Reid memorial lecture was to be on "Irish Traditional Music in France, An Exported Anomaly."

By Saturday lunchtime, the street signs of Ennis had been rewritten in French and Irish, and in glorious sunshine the two nations' tricolors were flying side by side in the breeze above the Old Ground Hotel. From an old-fashioned trumpet loudspeaker erected at the top of O'Connell Street, lively static-filled music was belting out over the town. As we turned into the street and passed the Poet's Corner pub, the winding narrow footpath was packed with people wandering in bright summer clothes. It was almost un-Irish, this weather, this gay warmth and light slanting over the rooftops onto the pink-skinned, freckled, and sunburnt crowds.

In a handful of pubs, musicians were already at it. Music oozed from open doorways, and in brown shadows the brief glistening of pint glasses flickered in pub darkness. There were tight, intimate little seisiuns already going on, and we might have gone in, sat down, and spent the afternoon in any one. For the moment, however, we had only come to sample the atmosphere, touch the mood of the fleadh, hear a first reel or two before coming back to Ennis that evening for the full traditional concert in the Danlann hall. So we did what most people do at fleadhs and wandered from the fading sounds of one seisiun into the swelling of another. Traffic in O'Connell Street was stopped by music. An open-sided lorry was parked before the statue of Daniel O'Connell, the Liberator, and seated along it were six musicians, young and old, fiddling, whistling, and drumming a reel. A large crowd had gathered around the lorry, there were young boys and girls from school sitting down on the street, old men were lined up along the walls and windows of Cash's clothing shop, babies were stopped in their prams and being rocked easily in the sunshine. The music played on, moving seamlessly from one reel into another. An old character in cloth cap, sweater, and tweed jacket hopped out on the street before the crowd. At first he stood absolutely still, then, an elbow rose, a shoulder swayed, a foot lifted and stepped, his head found the time and he was off on a dance. To cheers and laughter he was to-ing and fro-ing, hopping, stepping, even leaping, half-turning, moving an imaginary lady partner, being knocked a little out of step by her exuberance, winking at her, squeezing her, propping his hand firmly into the width of her back and "housing" her round the square in wild jigtime.

Up at the top of Abbey Street there were stalls set out with traditional instruments, and in the alley that ran between the street and the River Fergus, three men were crouched low around a new fiddle as its first notes fluttered delicately into air already alive with jigs from the square. In the crowds trailing up to the square there were dancers in traditional costumes, green tartans and black shoes, ready for the word. In a moment they'd be dancing hornpipes, high-stepping into the light of the afternoon. Until their turn arrived, I watched the dancing waiting inside of them, the coming of *their* fleadh, the clack, leap, and batter of steps just brimming within the muscles of their legs as they stood looking up at the lorry, nodding into the music, hands down by their sides, and waiting, waiting to dance.

By six that evening we were back in Ennis and had followed our ears to an open-air seisiun on the lawn before the Old

Ground Hotel. Here again was a gathering of people, a little milling crowd of listeners in the evening sunlight, standing around fiddles and a banjo while children ran around and skipped on the lawn. It was impossible to say how long it might have continued, for such seisiuns were almost by nature impromptu, sometimes starting at the chance meeting of two musicians who liked to sit in the same place, who shared a tune with each other. They began when they began, they stopped when they were finished.

We left the music playing behind our backs at half past seven and walked through the May evening light to the Danlann hall. We had no idea just what to expect from the Píob is Bodhran concert. *Píob* meant pipe, *bodhran* was a traditional drum instrument made of stretched goatskin. Was it to be three hours of pipes and drums then? As we walked up the road to the hall, still twenty minutes early for the stated starting hour of eight-thirty, there was a steady stream of people moving ahead of us. Having become used to events in Ireland starting anything from thirty minutes to an hour behind schedule, we were surprised. There were men, women, and children filing into the hall. In the parking lot, a girl of no more than twelve was getting into what appeared to be a French revolutionary costume.

Inside, the hall was packed and on the stage two rows of stools had been set out before a bank of microphones. The man next to me, eighty years of age, tapped his hand lightly upon his knee, as if the music had already started. The lights went down, and Labhrás O Murchú, chairman of Comhaltas Ceoltoiri na hEirinn, stepped onto the floor. We recognized him from our ceili at Cois na Habna, and recognized, too, the somewhat fierce way his speeches espoused the values of traditional Ireland: the family, the church, the music and dancing, and, of course, the language. He spoke first in Irish, and then in English, praising the unsung heroes of any fleadh, the behind-the-scenes men and women who brought the music into being, and the musicians who play for the love of it. Such people were the guardians of the national spirit in our music and our language, he said. And tonight, in a concert such as we were about to hear, the very best of Ireland would be on show. He left the stage to ringing applause, and a number of musicians started to filter out of the wings and move their stools an inch here, an inch there, until just right.

At the tap of three, the Liverpool Ceili Band launched into a reel. The music was on, the lights were low, and everybody's toes were tapping. There seemed no beginning, no middle, and no end. Once it was on and you were listening, the music took you inside it, a kind of endless rising falling diddley-idle-diddley-idle-diddley-idle-dee. It played on and on until a nod or a wink seemed to bring it to a halt.

We hadn't come out of the spell when the Kilfenora Jig was rising now with a heigh-ho-diddle-dee-idle-dee. They were *simply* brilliant, as the old man next to me said, putting the emphasis strangely on the first word not the second, and making me suddenly wonder whether Irish music was in fact simple or the incredible complex pattern of circles of sound that were still ringing in my ear.

There was only the slightest pause for thought. I looked at Chris. The heat in the hall was rising, and her face was flushed. Up at the back behind us there was a crowd of people jockeying around the door to look in, others were outside, sitting on the school steps, enjoying the May evening and listening. The lights went down again. Mick

Coyne, an Ennis man playing with Liverpool, hunched low over his Uileann pipes and squeezed a slow air. It was murmurous and sad, a music full of loneliness and melancholy that seemed to float out into visions all mists and hillsides, ancient and Gaelic, with a loveliness and sensuality that wrapped itself around the air. Here, in the low plaintive music of the pipes, was all the history and geography of Ireland mingled, here the windy mountain pass in Kerry, the desolate road in Connemara, the man in the rain mist walking home after the cows, the woman in the headscarf forking hay in the meadow. In the slow notes of the air was the spirit of the whole island. You could feel the Irish in it. We sat in a trance. There was no sound anywhere but for the quivering moan of Mick Coyne's Uileann pipes.

Sunday afternoon at two-thirty the Fleadh Nua Cultural Parade took off from Lifford Road. Twenty or so floats, some of them carefully representing the theme of "France and Ireland," began their long slow crawl through the narrow, crowded one-way streets of Ennis. In one lorry a mock guillotine had been mounted, and as the float passed up Abbey Street, a distinctly West Clare brand of French aristocrat was forced under the blade. Behind it were a pair of giant snails, slow-wiggling over by the crowd, and farther back still, beyond brass bands and marching groups of different branches of Comhaltas, the twelve-foot billowing sails of three great French warships and General Humbert and his luckless army of 1798, swaying through the streets of Ennis as if storm-tossed on the sea.

We heard the music of the next float before we saw it. Seated across the middle of an open-sided lorry was the

Liverpool Ceili Band once more, Sean Mac, Tom, Mick, and the others having by now, on Sunday afternoon, played a hundred tunes for the people of Ennis.

That evening, as the sun set at ten-thirty in a sky fabulous with golden light and empurpled cloud, we went to see them again. There was a ceili in the Queens Hotel. All afternoon we had been trying to get a set together. Dr. Harty was away at a conference; it was the beginning of the busy part of the farming year. Then, at short notice, our good friends Gerry and Liz Finucane said they'd come for the craic. They didn't know the figures very well, they had warned us. It didn't matter, we said, as long as they'd dance opposite us, I'd call the movements to them—anything for a set.

In the ballroom of the Queens Hotel at half past ten there were no more than a dozen people. Our old friends now, the Liverpool filed out on time, settled themselves, and started up. There had seemed to be nobody there, and yet, suddenly, there were six sets on the floor for the first figure. By the time the figure ended, the ballroom was filling steadily. And by the time the full set ended the place was abuzz with dancers. I marveled at how they had appeared out of the very walls. There was an earnestness in their faces, a sense of intentness, the wish to be out there hopping lively to the music. Two girls of twelve sat at a table in front of us drinking an orange drink, then got up, in party dresses, to dance the Siege of Ennis round the room, whirling cheerily about with men who might have been their grandfathers.

Somewhat timid, we, too, had sat out the first set.

"Next set?" I asked.

We all held hands in a ring, the drummer tapped thrice, and then one two and a onetwothree, and we were off. The floor spun to the music and in the spinning there were no cares or troubles, no sorrows or regrets. We were all moving together, every set halving and housing at the one time, every advance and retreat as mindlessly, effortlessly beautiful as waves on a shore. There was truly magic in this, and if across the six feet of our set the instructions sometimes got muddled, and the figure got fuddled a while, with panic and laughter, it always came together in time and rhythm. And when the two halves of the dozen sets all came in together with a great yell and thump, the hall floor sprung with the fun of it, and you felt everybody was one.

In the fine weather we set out for our first real cycling expedition. Bicycles to Doolin, then on to the Aran Islands. I am writing tonight in the sitting room of Mrs. Moloney's Horseshoe Bed and Breakfast. Exhausted. Sore bum. Niall and I set off early this morning, a glorious cool sunny day, two free wheelers. Thirty-five or so uphill miles, and the longest spell either of us had ever spent on the saddle. We had our rain gear secure inside our panniers. Soda water. Biscuits. Sweets for Niall. Two bananas and an orange. Sunglasses. Sunscreen. One map. A roll of toilet paper.

On the quiet empty road to Miltown Malbay I noted an abundance of images: Bird song like children's laughter.

White calf lying in the sun. Blown fields of bog cotton. Sunken car with hens inside. Yellow flags by the stream. Foxgloves. Always the scent of the sea. On the bicycles we see and experience the landscape in a completely different way. Niall says he smells cattle coming round a bend before he sees them. The smells are what we cycle through in this landscape, luxuriant, aromatic, fabulous, and quiet. We reached Lahinch without any difficulty by twelve, well ahead of schedule, and stopped for lunch at Liscannor. Then the uphill slog by the Cliffs of Moher to the bend in the road where the sea suddenly appears again. "There's Doolin!"

And out there, for tomorrow, is Inisheer.

This morning Lucy, Deirdre's godmother, drove over, bringing Deirdre to Doolin to join us. We cycled down to the pier, unloaded, and watched the horizon for the ferry. Inisheer, or Inis Oirr, means the easterly island in Irish. It lay like a low gray hill out there in the sea before us. A week previously, I had been told over the phone that the ferry ran every hour. But when I asked at the pier, the lady at the small ticket office said, "Well, it goes over once in the morning, and once in the evening, for sure. Be here at eleven-thirty."

So we were. But after an hour's wait on the pier brought no sign of the ferry, we cycled into the village for lunch. "It goes most days," said another woman up at O'Conor's, where sandwiches and soup were waiting for us. I wondered for a moment if there wasn't a conspiracy afoot, for certainly they seemed to have been expecting us there. At one o'clock the word was out: The Doolin ferry for Inis Oirr was on its way; it would be going back at half past one.

Back to the pier then, where we spotted a tiny crest of surf in the far sea that Chris called our ferry. There was a little gang of us assembled now, fifteen or so, Americans, Irish, and French, looking out expectantly at the compact little ferry bouncing toward us over the water. Only six of us carried luggage, the rest would return at the whim of the captain and the tide. An islander, all cap, narrow eyes, and no teeth, was dropped off by a midwestern Health minibus. He walked, poor-legged, to a huge rock and rested, deliberately not looking seaward. Illness had brought him off the island, and with a cigarette burning at the tips of his fingers he seemed to look at us all with a kind of mild dislike, as if none of us could really understand his life in his home.

The ferry pulled into the pier. A small white boat with the name *Tranquillity* hand-painted on its bow, it had a cabin full of life jackets and three wooden benches outside on deck. Minutes after we had loaded the bicycles on board, the engine roared and what had seemed from the pier the slowest, easygoingest ferry service in the world was now a bouncing, thrashing boat, running full-throttle into Atlantic currents. In a moment we were all holding on. Beneath a pale clouded sky a green-gray sea rose and fell sideways. Deirdre's face, one minute all curiosity and interest, was now white with shock. She began a whimper that would last almost the whole journey, until, sea-sprayed and exhausted, she fell asleep in Chris's arms as we came in to Inis Oirr.

There was a girl with red hair and black clothes standing

quietly by the railing, looking out at the tip of the island. There was something about her: She was a native. However long she had been away didn't seem to matter. There was something in the way she stood still through the battering of sea. The rest of us were giddy or apprehensive, sickly or clinging, first-timers for Aran, travelers lured by literature or legend, journeying across a churning sea to a place that existed, as yet, in the mind alone.

If in Ireland, be in Aran, an old Irish saying went. For if you spent any time on the island of Ireland, sooner or later your eye would turn westward, out there, to those three pieces of land swimming in gray waters at the end of Galway Bay. Out there was a world unto itself, a mythic place, a place hewn out of limestone and almost entirely without trees, a place where the fields had had to be man-made, millions of stones picked off them, and mounded composts of seaweed and sand brought from the shore. A place inhabited since prehistory, Christianized in the fifth century by St. Enda and then celebrated for cloistered holiness, a saints' sanctuary, which for whole months in winter was veiled from the world in rain. The Aran Islands, Hy Brasil, the Isle of the Blessed, invaded, pillaged, and garrisoned from the time of Queen Elizabeth through Cromwell and exploited on up to the 1920s when the island was returned to the islanders. Through all that, Irish survived as the language of Aran. Pride was out there, the fierce Irishry of fishermen rowing narrow black-bottomed curraghs in the heaving waters and surviving the harshness of life on islands necklaced with rosaries of stone.

The Aran Islands towered in my imagination. As I sat or stood, swaying in the sideways motion of the ferry and looking out at the Inisheer lighthouse on the tip of the island, I was filled with awe. I was approaching, in reality, a dream I had had since my school days, formed by a handful of plays and a book of travels written at the turn of the century by John Millington Synge. Synge was one of my heroes, and one of Chris's favorite Irish writers. In a famous moment of Irish literary history, W. B. Yeats, upon meeting Synge in Paris, had urged him to go to Aran and "express a life which had never found expression." Within twelve months, Synge had visited with the islanders, learned Irish, and found in their lives the inspiration for some of the finest works in Irish literature, among them, the plays *The Playboy of the Western World* and *Riders to the Sea,* and the account of his travels, *The Aran Islands.* I had a copy of it in my bag and knew the first lines by heart; "I am in Aranmor, sitting over a turf fire, listening to the murmur of Gaelic that is rising from a little public-house under my room."

Deirdre was asleep in her mother's arms as we passed the southern end of Inisheer, heading for the pier. At the tip of the island I saw a man with a small pony and trap emerge, an inch of head and horse showing above stone walls as he rode down the coast road to meet us. That man knows this ferry, I thought. He knows the exact watermark on this crossing from Doolin, the moment to rise from his chair, ready the horse, and set out to meet us. The horse's quick-trot along the white sands of the small beach was a measure of our nearness to the pier. He arrived as the ferry thumped and banged against old tires along the wall. There was a flurry of excitement among the passengers. We stood up and swayed, waiting the last moments. Chris took Deirdre; I, the bicycles. From the ferry to the island was a steep rise of quite narrow stone steps, part eroded on the seaside, and, without a railing, a drop of several feet into the tide. As the boat bumped to and fro, you picked your moment, made a little leap to the first step and climbed up. I was to hoist the bike overhead. I was shown how to get it over the narrow shiprail, and then carry it up. And so, in this way, with a bicycle up in the air over my shoulder, the front wheel turning in the breeze, I stepped off the boat and onto the Aran Islands for the first time in my life. It was my thirty-first birthday.

Inisheer is a little over two miles wide and two miles long. Nearly the entirety of its population live on the northeastern edge, looking past Black Head on the Clare coast into Galway Bay. There are five of what might be called town-ships, or communities: an Baile Thios, meaning the town below; Baile Lurgáin, midways up from the pier; Baile an tSéipéil, where the church is; Baile an Chaisleáin, domi-nated by high ruins of an old cashel (fort) wall and tower house; and Formna, the place of the top, or ridge, of the hill. In all not a mile separates them, and the rest of the island stretches emptily, hushedly, back to the south and west.

As we made our way up from the pier on a bright breezy June afternoon, Inisheer was quiet and closed in on itself. The area around the pier was dismal and unlovely; there were scattered beer bottles and other rubbish strewn here and there, the smell of burning plastic was sour on the air. And there was no bin anywhere. Curraghs lay upside down on the sand, with nets, old ropes, broken cages, rusted cans, and other bits and pieces laying around them. No one hired the pony and trap, and the man rode off back along the beach road, clucking through his teeth.

I felt extraordinarily disappointed, and kept trying to

thrust away my first impressions, to move them into a far corner of my mind, as I pushed the bicycles up a little sloping road to Óstan Inis Oirr — the ten-room hotel where we were to stay the night.

It was a simple, plain place — a bar and lounge; a comfortable, homey sitting room with a turf fire; a restaurant of a dozen tables with steak, lamb, salmon, mackerel, or pollack for dinner; an upstairs all white with timber doors; no pictures, posters, or photographs anywhere, just simple, plain white walls and a sloping roofline; a bathroom at the end of the corridor. Simple but fine. A bed, a wash basin, a roughly made wooden bedstand — it felt a little like an island cell, it suited me fine.

When we checked in, I sat down, trying to come to terms with my feelings of unease.

"There's no excuse for untidiness like that down around the pier," said Chris.

"Perhaps there is," I said. "Perhaps there's no easy way to get rubbish off the island."

"But it doesn't show pride. I don't understand it. I thought they cared so much about their islands."

"I don't know," I said. "I think they do, but maybe down around the pier is tourist ground, that's where the day-trippers come in, that's not the island proper, *their* island." It was an invented excuse, but it would do for the time being. Earlier in the day, over a massive breakfast in the Horseshoe B&B in Doolin, we had sat alongside a party of eight English tourists. One of them, speaking casually, had said to Chris, "There used to be twice as many people living here, right?" He went on to express his regret at the demise of the old farmhouse holiday, with chickens in the kitchen, thatch on the roofs. What they wanted, Chris said to me later, was designer poverty in Ireland. On Inisheer, then, *we* wanted no such thing. We wanted to find vibrancy and pride.

We went downstairs and got instructions from Kevin at the bar. Early in the afternoon, with Deirdre in her babyseat and Tim Robinson's indispensable map of the island in Chris's bike pouch, we set off to find the truth about Inisheer.

It was bright and warm and hazy with thin soft clouds sailing the pale sky. We took the road by the beach, hoping to make a circular ride around the perimeter of the island. Along the sand were little clusters of boys and girls of thirteen or fourteen walking, running, chasing the waves. All along the rising road between the sea and the hill of Formna we passed groups of them, with the bright friendly choruses of their *Dia dhuibh*s fluttering in the air. The Gaeltacht summer school on the island seemed to be thriving; packs of children speaking Irish greeted all comers with a kind of confident bravado, showing how easily phrases of the language suited them. As we bicycled slowly past them, they smiled at our returned *Dia is Muire dhuibh,* giggled sometimes at the shared exchange, and walked on in a gaggle of the gaelige. If the old men we passed on Inisheer seemed closed and unfriendly, these children made up for them. Every time you saw them, you felt the spirit of the place, for the mood of Inisheer on this June day was not created by fishermen and curraghs, Synge's nineteenth-century peasant men and women in rough tweeds and wool, but was made of children's voices and Irish words, a place of youth in summertime.

Beyond Formna, we climbed past the last of the houses, out of earshot of the young voices, and looked giddily downhill into the tremendous hush of the rest of the island. Those roads. What roads! None wider than eight feet, some narrowing to three, grass-covered, and running between shoulder-high stone walls. There was no vista, no view anywhere that was not ringed in these walls. There were hundreds of them everywhere you looked. The fields they embraced were the smallest I had ever seen, some, little meadows of thirty feet or so, immaculately walled on all sides. The tiny Aran fields are largely without gates. They have to be opened and closed by the moving of stones. Across a view of fifty yards and nearly as many walls, a man going down the road was only a head and shoulders, breasting silently forward as if through a sea of stone. There were of course no cars on the island, and as we pedaled at our ease through the winding, narrow maze, I realized these roads were the most *human* anywhere. They were made and still existed for people, not machines, and an extraordinary peace was locked inside their labyrinth. You could travel on and on, coming upon nothing but more walls and minute meadows, with the sea all around.

We found that there was no circular route around Inisheer. We would cycle down a long stony road to within a hundred yards of the sea, until the road itself disappeared into rough rock and limestone. Then we were forced back again, often to a point midway to the village, until a path, a grassy track, broke off to the right, winding bumpily upward only to arrive at another long stretching road south. Again the same thing would happen. The road would end before it reached the cliffs, becoming more and more rocky until at last you climbed off the bike and admitted it had gone. Back again then, on another boreen curving weirdly like a jigsaw piece, perhaps no wider than the bicycle itself but with shoulder-high walls on either side of it, and then out onto another road running southward.

In the foreword to Tim Robinson's map, he explains the evolution of this intricate island field and road system in two ways. The natural fissures in the limestone itself, which run in a south-southwesterly direction, have dictated the main roads, with side roads joining them in a kind of dancing zigzag. And then, in the path system is a clue to the history of the Aran islanders' life. For seaweed brought from the shore and mounded on quarter acres of ground where a thousand stones had been picked up to clear the earth was the main way soil was built up for the growing of crops. In earlier years seaweed was also sold to iodine factories on the mainland. Seaweed *rights* were established by the ancient division of the islands into thirty-six *ceathrúna* or "quarters," each of which ran north-south to the shore, each with a boreen for carrying the seaweed, which is still used today for moving animals along the edges of the quarters. There was no need for roads to run all the way to the cliffs; nobody went circleways, but up and down from the villages on their own rights-of-way.

So, back and forth we cycled Ceathrú an Locha, Ceathrú an Caisleáin, Ceathrú Droim Arlamáin—those timeless empty roads, clean gray threads unspooling to the sea. Sometimes, peering from the higher vantage of the bicycle, a tiny walled field revealed itself as a potato garden, and there, in the shelter of a high wall, without a house or cottage in sight, and surrounded by a maze of like fields, were perfect ridges of blossoming stalks.

We cycled as close as we could to the sea, and in late afternoon left the bikes where the road ended and clambered out, with Deirdre, on the great rocks of the southern foreshore, gazing across to the cliffs of Clare. Seabirds scattered into the air, the Atlantic beat softly, spending itself on the rocks with a gentleness that almost drew you to dive into the water that, they said, was warmer here than anywhere in Ireland. I watched the sea for nearly an hour, coming and going, foaming on the rocks, while Chris showed Deirdre the magic sand sifted from miniature shells.

It was certainly true what Chris said: that there was a sense of *us* and *them* on the island, which at times made you feel you were invading someone else's ground. It was partly the Irish, for in the language was the vocalized expression of Aran's otherness, the sound of stones in its mouth, and I wished again my Irish was better. Partly, too, it was the history of the place, the sense of difference that it had developed through centuries of having to endure on its own. Now Aran needed tourism to survive, even though tourism would end the uniqueness of its way of life. The houses on Inisheer today are a mix of old thatched cottages and modern bungalows. In another twenty years you might see holiday homes on this empty, stony southern shore.

At half past ten in the evening I slipped from the hotel back door and walked out around the village in the dying light. I followed the narrow roads where they led me, walking in the Aran quiet. *In* the road means something here, you feel you are truly inside a channel, a way, curving and rising, lovely and intimate, snug and self-contained. Round by little gardens of potatoes I walked and heard the jabber of Irish down by the pier, where a boat bringing Fianna Fail posters for the coming election had landed. *Dia duit. Dia dhuibh.* The herd of eight or so donkeys we had seen earlier up the hill had now come down to the water. Three sheep, roaming the roads, wandered into a cottage garden and were shooed out in the semi-darkness by a small boy. "Amach, amach," he called; then he saw me, and smiled. Up by the church with the little stone stiles in the walls, the sound on the night air was of ceili music. In the hall, the boys and girls at the Gaeltacht were having a dance. The stamp of feet in unison sounded over the village louder than the music. I could hear it all the way back to the pier. The light behind the ruined cashel wall faded into an inky blue, and I watched for stars but saw none.

Inisheer, Inisheer, I said softly to the darkening air, and then walked home trying to be quieter than my footsteps.

You're not to be too romantic about Aran, Chris had warned me earlier that morning in Doolin. This evening, when I came back from my walk, she went out.

"This is a wonderful place, I want to stay here," is what she said when she came back.

But Deirdre turned sick during the night, and we decided to return to the mainland the next morning. We had planned to travel on by boat to Inis Maan, the middle island, to see Synge's cottage there and the mound of stones by the sea's edge that he made his chair. But we were too concerned about Deirdre to go on. Rain poured down, the sea was choppy, and so the pleasures of the rest of Aran had to be deferred.

It was, fortunately, only a cold. Two days later, home in the prosaic world of Kiltumper, Deirdre is back to normal and so, too, are we.

· Chapter Seven ·

*Summer is a fine season for long journeys—Cuil
Aodha—Kenmare, village of our courtship—Italian
gardens on an Irish island—A night in Bantry House*

In Kiltumper, by mid-June, we had already begun calling
this our finest summer in five years. The days stretched in
long blue hours, warm and dry, into still bright bird-song
nights. Tractors in meadows drove until dark, past eleven
o'clock, hay trams stippled every view and the west of
Ireland became a sunny idyll more Greek than Gaelic,
shimmering yellow and gold in summer light. We counted
two weeks without rain, then it misted a day, and then the
sunshine came again. For the first time since our arrival
vegetables and flowers began to wilt in the ground, and

Deirdre ran giddily in and out the open front door wetly assisting with the watering can.

In the eleventh century there was an Irish saying, "Fó sín samrad síthaister," summer is a fine season for long journeys. And so, two days after midsummer day, hay in the barn and turf home, we loaded the car, put Deirdre (full of objections) into the babyseat, and took off on a summer jaunt.

We had mapped a circular route, a ring of four hundred miles, through the south. As the most common experience of travel in Ireland is in doing Bed and Breakfast, that was how we decided to go. In Kerry we would stay in Kenmare, a favorite haunt of ours, and then we would stop in Bantry, a place we had only driven through on the way to southwest Cork.

The hedgerows were already thick with fuchsia blooms and wild roses, and the ditches high with foxglove and daisies. The whole Clare countryside was bright with the colors of summer as I held onto Deirdre standing at the railing of the Killimer ferry, looking back at Clare. We crossed the Shannon River beneath a sky swift with white cloud, stepping onto Kerry soil in sunlight, and started down the now familiar route to Tralee and on into Killarney.

In 1749, Killarney was described as "this miserable village," and to Thackeray in 1842 it was "a hideous row of houses" beyond his carriage window. Today it is the most bustling tourist town in Ireland, a place of gift-and-souvenir shops. Its popularity derives from the changeless beauty of its three nearby lakes. People have been coming here since the mid-eighteenth century. Indeed, it might have been the town that invented tourism in the west of

Ireland, for as the road winds out of Killarney and past the line of horse-drawn jaunting cars and their jarveys, the traveler is swept into a landscape of luxuriant greenery, high mountains, and blue lakes. The civilized world—the world of cities—is left far behind. It's touring country in a very exact sense, a countryside to travel *through*. Once you leave Killarney you're into the thick of it, into a wilderness (fewer than ten houses in twenty miles) so idyllic and majestic that the road almost seems to take one on a tour of Eden. As if the scenery were not enough, in the eighteenth and nine-teenth centuries horse-drawn coaches clattering out these mountain roads were often accompanied by a little troupe of buglers whose occupation it was to blow trumpets and French horns along the ride so that the traveling ladies and gentlemen whom they were escorting might witness the Elysian effect of the Killarney echo. They blew their horns and the beautiful clear notes came back to them across the emptiness of the lake valleys—music of the heavens. As we drove it was easy to imagine carriages rattling and clopping along the curving summer road with the great tall trees rising on the left and the bluish glint of sky in the lakewater below. The rhododendrons have bloomed massively here forever. The murmurs, once heard from within horse-drawn carriages, are the exclamations—and snapshots—from rent-a-cars today. The place swaggers with majestic beauty, flaunts every hue and color: purple, blue, green, and gray on a hillside in sunlight; rose, russet, brown, and gold in the evening and in the shadows of passing clouds. These mountains of Ireland have a lofty nobility and the road through them is all edge and drop, with sweeping pan-oramic views falling away into the serene crystal of the lakes. The eagles that were so plentiful here a hundred years ago have vanished, but from a dozen green sleeping islets in the distance, clusters of birds swoop low over the water.

The road is narrow (wide enough for two "carriages," but small ones), and as we traversed the winding way slowly Deirdre grew impatient and then carsick, bringing us to a sudden urgent stop at Lady's View. Did they get motion-sick in eighteenth-century carriages, I wondered? Chris worried that Deirdre's supply of clean clothes would dwindle too quickly and advised me to drive even slower.

The trip over the mountain from Killarney to Kenmare became an age in itself. We crawled forward in second gear at a pace somewhat slower than a horse's trot, lingering over views we would otherwise have barely glimpsed, conceiving a greater respect for the mountains. By the time we drove into the village of Kenmare, Deirdre was banging at the car window ready to be let outside.

Mrs. Dignam was not at home when we reached her lovely house behind the trees at "Glendarragh," where we had booked for the night. The seven-year-old boy who opened the door to us pointed up the stairs to two spacious bedrooms with skylights, and then went off about his business. There was a nice casualness about it, an easygoing sense of holiday. Then, leaving Deirdre with a babysitter, Chris and I got back in the car to make a trip I had been planning since New Year's Day.

"Cool A," we had called it in the summer of 1973. I was fifteen then, a pale gangling Dubliner come to the Gaeltacht to improve his Irish. A train had taken us from Dublin, forty or so boys pushing, teasing, laughing in a carriage, waving goodbyes to a platform of parents as the train slid away, going down to bogland, as we thought of it, saying "Cork" to each other in Cork accents, eating crisps and chocolate bars and drinking red lemonade. It was my first true trip away from home, my first journey into my own identity. All my memories of it are crammed with a sense of fear and excitement. I remember arriving in Cork City, moving in a gaggling, whispering group under the eye of a Christian Brother into a bus. First, to Macroom, and finally on to the tiny village of Cuil Aodha in the heart of the west Cork Gaeltacht. I remember us piling out of the bus at last in the middle of the road that ran through the village, looking nervously around, pushing, whispering, wondering in dismay: Was this it? Was this deserted bend in the road and handful of houses what we, so full of the sense of adventure, had come to find? To us, "jackeens" from Dublin, there seemed to be nothing here.

We were there for a month. In groups we were boarded at different houses through the village. In the mornings we clattered down to a big rough wood table, said grace in Irish under the scrutiny of the Bean an Tí, the woman of the house, and then watched as she brought cuts of bread and homemade jam, two pots of tea, and hot plates of breakfast fry to the table. Afterward there were Irish classes in two prefabricated buildings down near the church. They lasted until noon, then back to Bean an Tí's for midday dinner, after which there was gaelic football on a bumpy, hoof-pocked field, or swimming in the waist-high river. In the evenings there were indoor games. We played chess and tabletennis. On weekends there was the stamp and cheer of ceilis in the hall. Through every day, evening, and night we spoke in Irish. It was widely rumored that a boy had been sent home the previous year for being caught speaking

English and although we did, too—in whispers and lone moments—all exchanges in public, whether on the field, in the river, in the shops, before the priest or the Bean an Tí were entirely in Irish.

Cuil Aodha, Cool A. The day we arrived we had thought it the most uncool place in the world. Nothing but mountains, green fields, and the untraveled road through the village on which nobody seemed to come or go. And yet . . . it had stayed with me, hadn't it? Something had started in me, there. Still, driving to it from Kenmare in midafternoon, I was almost afraid to see it again.

No one else could truly share my feeling, for what I revered in remembering Cuil Aodha, I realized, was my own innocence. Here, for me, a moment between childhood and manhood had been frozen. It was filled with the sounds of Irish, now nearly lost to my adult tongue and only slowly returning. It was filled with my first delight in being part of the countryside of Ireland. I was returning to an earlier self.

We passed Kilgarvan, Morley's Bridge, and journeyed into the shadow of the Derrynasaggart Mountains. We drove on in silence through green hills overhung with clouds. The scenery had a vague familiarity, or so I told myself, like a slowly developing photographic print. Then Chris pointed out the river down in the valley on our left. Was this the same river? Two miles later, driving now as slowly as possible, we crept past the sign in Irish that welcomed us to Cuil Aodha. And then, true to memory, I saw the farmer's field with the sweep of mountains at its back that had been our football pitch and heard the Gaelic cries and shouts of boys chasing a ball. A goal was a *cul* and a point a *cuilín,* which sent the goalie wading across the river to retrieve the ball. A cluster of boys in summer shorts had played on this field, in this timelessly beautiful setting of mountain and valley. Yet it seemed to me that game of football would go on forever. Wherever my classmates had disappeared to around the world—Mick O'Neill, Richard Healy, Conor Harrington, Rory O'Halloran—surely the mention of the name Cuil Aodha would conjure them instantly here to this rough field in Irish summer.

We drove slowly on into the village. There was the ceili hall and the *siopa* for sweets, the church, the *Oifig an Phoist* for letters home, and the parcel place where my mother in mid-month sent a favorite fruit cake, among whose ingredients was stewed tea. It had caused a midnight riot as boys sneaked past the Brother's room over the creaking floor to cut crumbling chunks of it with a pencil. I remembered.

We parked the car in front of the ceili hall. Across the road in a little garden in front of her house a white-haired woman was kneeling to weed.

"Go talk to her," Chris urged me, "go on. Speak Irish, Niall. And ask about Sean O'Riada."

I was reluctant to break my mood of nostalgia. But Chris was eager to see the house here in Cuil Aodha where the Irish composer Sean O'Riada had brought his family in the early sixties, devoting himself to his idea of "the Gaelic nation"—Irish language, music, and culture. He had become our foremost composer, producing a handful of important classical works, influenced by Greek literature in a way similar to Joyce and late Yeats. Then, invited to compose a score for the Gael-Linn documentary film, *Mise Eire,* he had successfully translated authentic Irish traditional music into symphonic terms, and changed Irish music forever. From Cuil Aodha he organized an orchestra of traditional musicians called Ceolteoiri Chualann, and at a time when traditional music in Ireland was at its lowest ebb of popularity, confined largely to dance bands or solo playing, he inaugurated a new era. In a country whose musical development was a chaos of two entirely separate traditions—one ancient and Gaelic, rejecting academic style and looking to Carolan (the great eighteenth-century blind harpist); the other, international, scholarly, and largely connected to city life and the Anglo-Irish ascendency—Sean O'Riada had managed a kind of synthesis. By the time of his death, in 1971 at the age of forty, Irish music had achieved a new life. The music he wrote for a Mass in Irish is heard all over the country today. His son, Peader, who lives in the family home in Cuil Aodha, is the leader of the Cuil Aodha Men's Choir, a powerful and excellent group of singers we had heard several times since coming back to Ireland.

"Dia duit," I greeted the woman who was weeding.

"Dia is Mhuire dhuibh," she gave us back, blessing us in words in saying hello. She stood up slowly.

"Niall MacLiam is ainm dhom," I began, falteringly, trying to find the words with which to tell her in Irish that fifteen years previously I had studied here. She smiled warmly as I went on, taking my reappearance as a kind of praise. Her name, she said in English, was Bean ui Cotter. She had ten boys staying at the moment. When I described the house, she told me I had stayed at Bean ui Shuilleabhain's. It was just down the road, but Bean ui Shuilleabhain had since gone. Somebody else lived there now and opened her home to the students.

"And do you speak Irish all the time?" Chris asked her.

"I do," she said. "We all speak Irish to the boys. In the shops and on the road and that, we all speak Irish."

"Does everyone in Cuil Aodha?"

"Yes, everyone does while they're still in national school. Then when they have to go away to secondary school, of course, it's English they're hearing mostly and talking it, too. It's dying out, the Irish, you know."

"It was said to be dying out a little bit fifteen years ago," I said.

"Yes, that's true," said Bean ui Cotter with a bit of a smile. "They're always saying that." She was a lovely gentle woman. She answered all my questions, told us where Sean O'Riada had lived—the white house under the trees that Chris had already spied—only a hundred yards or so beyond the house where I had stayed. I knew nothing about him then, of course. I had sung his Irish Mass at the very heart of its creation in the Cuil Aodha church without the slightest idea of who had written it.

We said goodbye and drove down the road. At O'Riada's house I pulled over and we looked in through an ivy-covered gate at a rise of stone steps and a great shaggy Irish wolfhound gazing out at us. He stared at us with a knowing look that was at once friendly and faintly humorous.

I remembered Bean ui Suilleabhain's on the road out of Cuil Aodha as a two-story house with pebbles in front of it and a view across the river into the green hills. The pebbles were gone now, the house seemed smaller, but the important thing was just the same. Here, in the stillness that stretched to the south under a blue Cork sky, was the same immensely hushed quietude, that pastoral emptiness that I had gazed out on in my boyhood, walking home to Bean ui

Shuilleabhain's, my ears humming with Irish words and Irish phrases, and my mind wondering what out there in all the wide world was I to become.

Back in Kenmare we walked with Deirdre around the pretty triangle of streets that make up one of our favorite Irish towns. Kenmare nestles in the crook between the outstretched arms of two magnificent mountainous peninsulas. It's a haven between the mountains, and its shops and restaurants are lively, bright, and decorative. Quinn's on the corner is a maze of woolen sweaters. The Purple Heather serves good food and is all bare stonework. Besides this, in the Park Hotel, the town boasts one of the finest hotels and restaurants in the country.

In the early evening, Deirdre safely asleep at Mrs. Dignam's with a baby-sitter listening for her, Chris and I slipped from the house for a second drive into memory. Once, ten years ago, on the mildest Valentine's Day anyone could remember, we two had taken a train from Dublin together and come courting into Kerry. Our stay was two days in a marvelous old house by the water. No one else was there, and with every place closed in February, the naturally secluded feeling of the house was doubled. We were our own Diarmuid and Grainne, reading poetry and escaping west into the green rush of early Irish springtime. We walked miles by hedgerows and ditches. We talked morning, noon, and night along country roads where daffodils were already rising, took knowing nods and salutes from passing farmers, and waved and saluted back in the growing knowledge that yes, truly, we would be married. Here, in a place not half an hour from Cuil Aodha, where I had stood, as a boy, gazing at the countryside, full of questions, had come one of the answers. Kenmare: courtship, love.

Under the glow of a midsummer sky, we drove west from Kenmare on the Sneem road to see if we could find that house by the water again. Chris and I remembered Marino House as a fine two-story building with a great sitting room and a roaring fire where we could sit and talk and take evening mugs of cocoa from a kind woman whose spirit had seemed fairy-godmother-like to both of us. As we drove out of town the whole feeling of the road along the peninsula came flashing back to us, its green richness, the sense of water, and the fragments of view through the trees of mountains and hills across the Kenmare River. We drove slowly, inching into our shared dream, and I felt the landscape conspire with our mood. This was a place of entrancement even if it had not already held a place in our hearts. The red and purple saucers and spires of wild fuchsia sprawled in high hedges. Teori De I had heard them called in Irish, the tears of God. By summer's end all roadsides would be edged red with their flowers, struck down by the rain. But for now they bloomed in a magical evening light as fine as any we had seen in Ireland. Under tree-shadows and by leaf-light, smelling the sea and the tangled woodbine, we at last found the long road into Marino House. It was almost a mile in from the main road, a narrow one-car track to the water's edge. We turned a bend and drove slowly up to the front of the house. And there it was, almost everything—the steps to the arched stone porch of the main door, the clinging ivy, the window, within which was "our" sitting room. The low sounds of water still lapped all around. The only thing that was different was the little cluster of foreign cars in the carpark. I pulled up at the side of the house and we sat there, unable to decide whether to go in or not. We sat outside and looked; then we drove away. That night in Mrs. Dignam's, with a light in the sky that seemed undying, I wrote: "First day of our jaunt, two drives to two places of memory, Cuil Aodha and Kenmare, Innocence and Love."

The following morning I awoke at a quarter past seven to find a four-year-old boy standing by the bed staring straight at me. His name, he said, was Michael. His daddy was sick, his daddy could only drink milk. Delivered of this burden, he charged out of the room and down the stairs into the kitchen. Deirdre, at first amazed, rapidly began to comprehend that this might be one of the joys of holidaying in someone else's house.

Mrs. Dignam's breakfast room had large glass windows and a lovely view down the wooded and rocky hillside to the water. Michael, another guest's child, disdained this, however, and insisted on being fed half in the kitchen and half in the hall. It says much for the open-minded and homey feeling of the household that he was quietly accommodated wherever he went, hiding his crusts for Mrs. Dignam to find later, crawling in the sitting room, dashing outside to tumble in the grass between mouthfuls. His father, not sick, not restricted to milk, shrugged his shoulders at us when Chris asked him how he was feeling. "He makes up things," he told us helplessly, watching the galloping figure of his son. We nodded as if we understood, and were thankful to be traveling with a Terrible Two, not a Fanatic Four-year-old.

Italian gardens on an Irish island. An irresistible prospect. On the way to Bantry from Kenmare our road passed through Glengariff. We decided to take a chance. Dressed in rain gear, we followed the signs down to the harbor to the boats bound for Ilnacullin on Garinish Island.

Ilnacullin in Irish means the island of holly. Before it was bought by a man named Byrce in 1910, the island was described as a goat-ridden reef of thirty-seven acres sitting in the middle of Glengariff Bay—an unlikely place for a garden paradise. But that is exactly what it is, one of the most spectacular gardens in Ireland. And the fifteen-minute boat ride is especially nice for a two-year-old. On the brown and black whale-back rocks, twenty or thirty seals were lying in the mist. Niall made a face like a seal, or should I say tried to make one, and showed Deirdre where the whiskers go. Deirdre, in turn, scrunched up her mouth and nose and shouted to the seals. Compared with our last boat ride, to Inisheer, this tranquil jaunt on the motorboat *Blue Pool* was luxurious.

Ilnacullin is a gardener's garden—magical. The ever-changing color of the mountains provides a natural yet unique backdrop for the hundreds of plants that flourish in the moist air and temperate climate here, aided by the

warm waters of the Gulf Stream. Glengarriff itself is surrounded on three sides by mountains. With the shelter
provided by Scotch and Austrian pine and even two wind-
resistant California conifers—Monterey pine and
cypress—Ilnacullin is a tiny sun trap. In keeping with the
enchanted setting of the place, as soon as we arrived the sun
came out. Perhaps the sun is drawn here, I thought, as we
walked around the beautiful flower-fragrant island, our
rain gear tied to our waists.

There is a teahouse with a reflecting pool surrounded by
Roman statuary, an Italianate bell tower, a Martello tower,
and a Grecian temple overlooking the sea. And, as the Irish
say, it is "chockerblock" full of exotic and tropical plants.
Secret spaces are connected by winding paths and stone
steps, and the scent of flowers and shrubs and trees is
everywhere.

Deirdre ran happily down the grass walk known as
Happy Way. Niall loved the rambling roses crawling over
bare rock. A white-flowering, silver-foliaged California
poppy shrub caught my eye. I was dying to take a snippet of
it for my own fledgling Kiltumper Cottage garden. If Byrce
was able to transport all this, including boatloads of soil,
onto this tiny island, then, surely, I should be able to grow
some more exotic plants. I was inspired.

Having read a little about it in the tourist board's "Historic
Houses, Castles and Gardens" pamphlet, Chris had chosen
Bantry House for our next night's stay. In mid-afternoon, in

a drizzling rain, we drove through Bantry town, around past the harbor, in through the gateway, and up to the former residence of the Earls of Bantry. First built around 1750, this beautiful, partly Georgian house at the head of Bantry Bay looked every inch an Earl's residence. Couched in its own grounds and Italianate gardens (now overgrown but under renovation) with the bay and the mountains off to the right, it had, at first, an air of cool aloofness as we unloaded our bags and stepped from the car to gaze at it.

"Oh, look, Deirdre. Look at this beautiful house. Deirdre's going to sleep in *this* house tonight. Won't that be fun?"

Fun? I was a little afraid of what welcome or lack of it there might be here for Deirdre. This was a Historic House, open to members of the public, who paid to wander among the collections of antique furniture and objets d'art. The house had only recently been opened for Bed and Breakfast, and at £25 per person it was fairly reasonable. In a little troupe, all bags and baby, we hurried up the steps out of the rain and inside to a reception desk where a man in an open-necked white shirt and faintly dusty blue blazer was listening to a transistor radio playing swing music as he collected £2 a person and handed out admission tickets.

He greeted us with a smile. And when I introduced myself and inquired about the rooms we had reserved, he turned off the music.

"Shall I show you the rooms, sir," he said in tones so full of politeness and welcome that I was almost taken aback.

"Yes, thank you." We followed as he led us inside the house, passing little clusters of men and women bent over chairs, pictures, and china with clipboard summaries describing the house's antiques. They glanced over mildly in our direction as the four of us were swept up the stairs and along a hall and into a great book-walled, high-ceilinged library. Our guide walked toward a far wall, reached for a handle that suddenly seemed to appear, and opened a concealed door, gesturing us into another wing of the great house. Deirdre, of course, was delighted by all this, and trotted through the "camouflaged" door with a laugh. We followed on again, up a flight of stairs, past a carpeted landing with television and three comfortable armchairs, and along a corridor to its end.

"Here is one room, sir," said the man, whom I had gathered, by now, was the owner of the house. He held open the door and we stepped inside it. Anything, I believe, would have suited us fine right then, anything, just to be staying the night inside this extraordinary place. As it was, the chamber to which he brought us took our breath away. There was a huge double bed, great armchairs, and a table with fresh flowers reaching four feet high and a massive bowl of dried petals. The room was shaped like an oval bowl with two windows. One window looked out on to the courtyard at the front of the house and out to the bay, the other faced east to the hillside overgrown with trees and shrubs—111 steps to the top, and a glorious view of a manicured lawn stretching down to the bay, crowned by white wrought-iron planters of geraniums and lobelia and many summer annuals. The bathroom was spotless and spacious. The whole room had an elegant air of graciousness, just like our host. It was refreshing and relaxing, something fine, genteel, and so civilized that we had no hesitation in declaring it the most pleasant room we had seen in Ireland. There had been other rooms, in castles and big hotels, that were perhaps larger, more dramatic, or more grandly furnished, but to us they had never seemed anything other than "show" rooms; you never felt anyone *lived* there. This room in Bantry House had a quality of welcome that made it seem like a home.

"I'm sorry to say, sir, that some guests yesterday broke our baby cot," said our host. "Perhaps your daughter could sleep on this low camp bed. She wouldn't hurt herself, even if she fell out," he added kindly, smiling over at Deirdre. "I'm very sorry about it, sir."

Although Deirdre had never slept a night outside a crib, I assured him that we would manage fine. He told me there would be a trolley of tea, coffee, milk, and biscuits, with an electric kettle, just outside the room for the afternoon and night, but if we chose there was a tearoom downstairs now open. He closed the door and left us. Chris jumped on the bed; Deirdre jumped on the bed.

After washing up we looked over our information about Bantry House and read that the owner was Mr. Egerton Shelswell-White, a direct descendant of the Earl of Bantry. Our host was a musician, who had been farming in Alabama when he received the news that he had inherited the family estate. He had returned with his wife and family and was now engaged in trying to keep it going in the face of the massive upkeep the house and grounds demanded.

We had been given our own key to the east wing, and unsure that we would be able to find our way back the way we had been brought, we let ourselves out on to the front courtyard, walked across the pebbles, and came in once more by the front door. Mr. Shelswell-White was back at his desk listening to melodic saxophone music. He greeted us with another smile.

"We wondered if you could show us the tearoom?" I said.

"Of course, sir, after your journey," he said. "Follow me." And again we were off, under the stairs, in a door, down a hall, past a bicycle, a babyseat, around a curving passage, through the kitchen where two girls turned to gaze at us in wonder as we walked past and out into the tearoom. "There you are now, someone will be in to see to you in a moment. When you want to go out, you can go out by the main entrance there, sir," he said, pointing to the door to the outside. The marvelous and eccentric tour through the bowels of the ancient house was, it seemed, only for guests guided by the owner himself, a man who walked in slippered ease through his home.

As we sat down to tea, I realized just how extraordinary our welcome into Bantry House had been. The magnificence of the house was obviously not lost on our host, but it was not of first importance. For droves of people wandered through it, and yet there was no obvious "security." This air of trust pervaded everything. After tea, Chris and I went around to the front door for the third time, and for the third time met our host at his desk, this time to set off on the "formal" tour of Bantry House.

It is quite a place. Turn right and you're in the Rose Drawing Room with high windows overlooking the bay where Wolfe Tone stood on the deck of a ship filled with French troops, stranded in a storm, unable to land. A four-panel Royal Aubusson tapestry hangs on the walls. It was made as a wedding present for Marie Antoinette. Over by the front window was a set of antique red and white chess pieces in their case, and a collection of birds' eggs with small labels handwritten in fading blue ink: the Golden Crested Wren's large, hand-sized egg; the Blue Tit's; the Green Linnet's; the Grey Rook's; the Yellow Hammer's; the Corncrake's. On an antique table, family photographs, a lineage of faces from the owner's mother and father to a grandfather to one speckled print of Margaret, Countess of Salisbury, 1473–1541, known as Blessed Margaret, beheaded on Tower Hill, London, "The Last of the Plantagenets," and the great-great-great-great-great-great-great-great-great-great-great-great-great-great-grandmother of Mr. Egerton Shelswell-White. In brackets beneath it: "To save you counting, there are fourteen greats."

In the Ante Room, with a William IV rosewood breakfast table in its center and on it a vase of fresh morning flowers from the garden, there was a feeling that someone might have breakfasted there that morning, using the family's breakfast service from the nearby display case in which we could also see the slight tarnish on a coronet which had been worn by the First Earl at the coronation of Queen Victoria. In the deep blue Dining Room, we stood in the door and looked the length of it, down through two massive gray marble columns; past Chippendale chairs, sideboards, and serving tables, a teapoy, wine bins, and a gold bust of St. Patrick to the royal portraits on the far wall. The long table in the center was set for twenty-four guests and stood frozen, Miss Havisham-like, in eternal readiness.

Back out then and into the Inner Hall, where a collection of curious odds and ends, tokens and memorabilia collected from the Earl's trips to Europe were set out on a black-and-white tile floor. Here among a cluster of other things was a Traveling Household Shrine with fifteenth- and sixteenth-century icons, brought from Russia by Viscount Berehaven; the faded standard of the Bantry Cavalry from 1778; a sixteenth-century Spanish marriage chest. A dark, sixteenth-century Mosque Lamp from Damascus stood

alone in the corner. The entire house—downstairs and upstairs, its drawing room, its dining room, its book-lined
library, its bedrooms and washrooms, its lobbies and
halls—was a family testament to continuity and tradition.
On an upstairs lobby wall were a number of illuminated
addresses:

> To the Right Hon. The Earl of Bantry,
> My Lord, We the inhabitants of Bantry and its neigh-
> borhood cannot allow this, your first visit since your
> Lordship's marriage and succession to the family title
> and estates, to pass by without expressing the heartfelt
> joy which we feel at seeing you once more among
> us. . . .

And whatever you felt about the troubled entangled history of Ireland, of lords and earls in a countryside of starv-
ing peasants laboring under penal conditions, it was hard in
Bantry House to deny a sense of satisfaction in being in a
place connected to its past. As neither of us were particularly knowledgeable about antique furniture or paintings, it
would have been easy for Bantry House to have seemed
stuffily complacent, a place where people came just to gog-
gle. But here history had fallen into the right hands, and the
benign, slightly eccentric spirit of the Shelswell-Whites
pervaded the place, and made Rooms into rooms. When the
night had drawn in it was comforting to gaze out from our
bedroom in the guests' east wing across to three upstairs
lighted windows in the main house where children were
playing. This great old house was still a family's home.

Was I walking or sleeping last night as I dreamed of ghosts? The good spirits of Bantry House disturbed my sleep only mildly, but I was certainly conscious of them. My little girl slept for the first time in a bed, not a cot, without once stirring from it. She slept like an angel warmly tucked in bed while guardian spirits watched over her.

This morning we took a side trip to Castletownsend, Cork. We drove through the dripping lush countryside of the Carberry coast to the village of the two trees. Castletownsend must have the steepest main street in Ireland. It descends on a curve dividing around two trees in its center, and slopes on toward the castle, a church, and a little harbor. As we drove its length in the drizzle I was disappointed that the old trees that I had seen fifteen years ago when I was a student had died. But two young saplings now stood in their places. Castletownsend is a ghostly sort of village. There was not a person in sight. It is an out-of-the-way place that doesn't get many tourists. But it is a beautiful spot and behind high, well-made stone walls elegant ivy-clad houses stand sleepily. It is a hushed place by the water redolent with the vestiges of Anglo-Irish charm. There is a blend here of the big houses of the Anglo-Irish Ascendency and the Irish village house. It is more like a village in England than Ireland, perhaps; but it is precisely the kind of village that one would expect to find from the stories of Sommerville and Ross, who wrote thirteen novels about Victorian Ireland, including *The Real Charlotte* as well as *Some Experiences of an Irish R.M.*, made into a recent television series.

Edith Sommerville lived at the top of the hill in Drishane House most of her life and died in her sister's house, Tally Ho. She was a most remarkable woman, a sportswoman who hunted and bred horses, a painter, and most notably, co-author with Martin Ross (Violet Florence Martin of Ross House, Co. Galway) her cousin, of entertaining but very astringent fiction.

Edith was also organist at St. Barrahane's Church. Fifty-two steps, one for every Sunday of the year, lead up to St. Barrahane's with its beautiful stained-glass windows by Harry Clarke, one of the great glass craftsmen of modern times. When Edith Sommerville died it was her wish to be buried beside Violet Martin in the churchyard of St. Barrahane's. On the day of the burial, the gravediggers discovered that Edith's chosen resting place was solid rock. Not wanting to deny the wish of so revered a woman as Miss Edith Sommerville, a local man was quietly dispatched in search of some dynamite. He returned and a hole was blasted for the coffin. But the cross over Miss Martin's grave was loosened by the explosion and it toppled askew to the horror and embarrassment of the gravediggers. A typical Sommerville and Ross anecdote.

· Chapter Eight ·

The road North—Newry—County Down—
Belfast at sunset—from the Glens of Antrim
to Giant's Causeway

Summer 1989 was made of long, hot, blue days of sunlight and stillness, of the garden in high blossom around the cottage, and rose blooms tumbling from the stone cabin walls. The ground baked drier than we had ever seen it. The days of summer 1989 are like memories of an idyllic childhood: up through the morning fields with the brush of tall grass on our bare legs, the immense white sky turning bluer by the hour, cows lying in shade by stone walls and white-thorn bushes, the heat in the ground and its hardness underfoot, the durable firm feel of summer against which the thought of mucked gaps and boggy fields seem to fade, air cross-hatched with the flight of birds and their song, the world paused in a dreamy warmth. Our days ended on bicycles, pedaling twelve miles to the evening sea at Spanish Point for foamy, salty, sensual swims in the in-coming tide, then home again.

It has been glorious. In the front and out the back door Deirdre ran, the spirit of the season, nappyless and carefree. We would sit outside on the bench in the morning and look away across the fields and think one summer like this was worth enduring three of wind and rain. Temperatures reached into the eighties in Ireland for the first time in several years. In the *Irish Times,* articles on the nation's hysterical rush to the seaside began to take precedence over those devoted to the inconclusive results of the general election. "Costa Del Dublin," read one headline, and there were daily photographs of behatted and short-trousered men and women sitting out on beaches as hot as those of Spain, pinking and freckling with the best of them.

In Kiltumper, we enjoyed bouquets of red poppies in glass vases and bountiful crops of fresh sugarsnap peas, broccoli, lettuce, and onions brought from the garden. The evening meal, with the faint wind rustling the shell chime in the kitchen window, became the richest meal of all, full of the simple rightness of bringing food straight from garden to kitchen. On our farm the animals thrived. On the fourth of July, in Upper Tumper on a flattened bed of rushes, Phoebe, our tidy Friesian cow, gave birth to twin calves, a shorthorn bull and a whitehead heifer. The idyll of Kiltumper seemed complete. But I reminded myself of the New Year's Day resolve to go in search of other Irelands beyond our bounds. From the heart of this idyll, then, to

Irish reality today. With Deirdre "going on her holidays" to Lucy and Larry, her Irish godparents, for four days, we two set off for Belfast and Ulster.

With the map of Ireland spread before us, we drove north toward Galway and turned off onto the Dublin road. We passed still lakewater and a handful of paddling swans. In Athlone, legendary center of Ireland, bright sailboats were moored in sunshine on the Shannon River. To the north was the inland sea of Lough Rea, and the sleepy town of Lissoy of which Oliver Goldsmith had written "Sweet Auburn, loveliest village of the plain, where health and plenty cheered the laboring swain. . . ."

We drove through the tidy but empty town of Ballymore to Mullingar and stopped for lunch: soup, chops, potatoes, and good old marrowfat peas. Good honest stuff, take it or leave it. The road took us out of County Westmeath into Meath: Clonmellon with tall trees growing in stone circle beds that were actually in the road, a few feet from the sidewalk; Kells (Ceanannus Mór in Irish), once a center of learning celebrated throughout Europe. St. Columba founded a monastery here in the year 550, leading two and a half centuries later to the superbly illustrated manuscript of the Gospels that is known as The Book of Kells. After Kells we passed through Ardee in County Louth. Here, every Irish schoolboy and girl is taught how Cuchulainn, champion of Ulster, fought from daybreak to sunset against Ferdia, his best friend, both of them retiring at nightfall to secretly bathe each other's wounds before resuming their fight in the dawn. Here in Ardee, at the bridge of Ferdia (Baile Atha Fhirdhia), Ferdia was slain.

After Ardee we drove through Dundalk. To the west was County Monaghan and the poet Paddy Kavanagh's village of Inniskeen, to the east the Cooley Peninsula, setting for the Ulster cycle myths of Cuchulainn and the *Tain Bó Cuilainn*.

Four hours brought us across the map of Ireland, to The Border, which runs from the Atlantic coastline to the Irish Sea. In ours, as in many travelers' minds, the middle of the island had seemed more a place to traverse than to linger in. We'd preferred the coast and sea air. But bumping northeastward across the country toward Dundalk and the Belfast road, we were made newly aware of the wealth of layered history and varied geography of middle Ireland. The drive itself seemed to lead us through a constantly changing panoply of poets and saints, heroes and warriors, lakewater and blue hills, rivers, green fields, and stone walls. In this unfrequented part of the country, in pastoral peace, we found, unexpectedly, green places full of secrets and beauty. We would come again to linger; this is what travel in Ireland is about.

We arrived at last at Ulster, The North, the Six Counties, the area that is known to the world as the place of "the Troubles." I had been there as a boy with my mother, up and down from Dublin on the train in the same day to shop in the big English department stores. English sweets, bars of chocolate, and toy English soldiers are what I remember — but that was long ago in a different age. Since 1969 all our television screens have brought us, protected, glimpses of the strife, of marches and riots, stone-throwing, fire-bombing, knee-capping, baton-charges, rubber-bullets, and tear gas. We have come to know of the Shankill and the Falls roads, read the familiar graffiti of a sectarian war, the three-letter-word daubings—IRA, UVF, and others—and to feel from the green tranquillity of southern Ireland, if only vicariously, the griefs of bombed shops, bridges, and roads "up North." But the truth is, the North is the North, and despite the two decades of internal war in Ulster, little of its anger or bloodshed has spilled into the rest of the island. That is a fact. Another, quoted in the London *Sunday Times* this March: There were three times more people murdered in Washington, D.C., last year than in the *whole* six counties of Northern Ireland, which has a similar population. And another fact, this from the Northern Irish Tourist Board, contains an important truth: "In twenty years we've never lost a tourist yet!"

Plainly put, the struggle in Northern Ireland is, and has been, largely between the Republican and Loyalist factions of its population. No attempts are made to ambush tourists.

All this said, such is the impact of newspapers and television that Chris's and my image of what we might expect once we crossed the border was certainly colored with the faint tinge of apprehension of violence. Dan, an American friend studying at Queens University in Belfast, had called earlier in the week to assure us that it was a wonderful city and that in the years he had been working on his doctorate he had never encountered trouble. I took his word and that of others, too, and, in leaving the peace of Clare for the North, had full confidence that we would spend four tranquil days in beautiful countryside. Well, nearly full confidence—we left Deirdre behind with friends.

At the border we saw our first British soldier. Helmeted, dressed in camouflage uniform, holding a small machine gun, he stood alone beyond the customs and police officers at the place where the North began. We slowed into a line of cars and waited. I imagined other soldiers somewhere beyond the walls and the little hills of grass, routinely watching us. A green-uniformed officer in a bullet-proof vest waved the cars to him, one by one, across a series of low ramps in the road. You bumped slowly forward and were either waved on or to one side as the officer on duty decided. As we sat there, next in line, Chris rummaged for our passports. Did Irishmen and women need passports to enter the north of Ireland? For a minute I wasn't sure, and despite all the assurances of safety I felt a little anxious. Like everyone else, we, too, had heard stories of cars stopped for hours, stripped down to their innards in detailed searches by unnervingly silent or coldly polite soldiers. It was our turn. Sunshine was beating down, and under the weight of his bullet-proof vest and gunbelt the man who motioned us to him was glistening with sweat.

"Going touring, sir?"

"Yes, just for a few days."

There was a pause, his eyes traveled across the backseat, our bags, our travel books.

"Carry on." A wave of his hand, a bump over another ramp, and we were in Northern Ireland.

At once we sensed change. The road was better, the signposts were different, newer, English-style, not Irish, and the feeling of space itself was different. It is extraordinary on so small an island, but immediately we felt we were in another country. Motoring on the smooth wide surface of the M1, we arrived at Newry and for a moment lost our way. We passed a road that was cordoned off and guarded by three Security Force soldiers. That unnerved us a bit. Especially when Chris shouted out, "Wait, that's our road, B24." It was, but, fortunately, going in the other direction.

I was glad not to have had to inquire of the soldiers what detour to take. The part of Newry we drove through was depressed and unpleasant. We passed a little boy dressed in green and black, like a little IRA soldier. He stood below a telephone pole bearing a poster of Sinn Fein. We went wrong at a roundabout and drove up a street where half the shops were shuttered and closed. A siren sounded down the road behind us, and I pulled the car over in a panic. Images from the television news flashed before us, of car chases, armored vehicles, bullets. But only a fire engine went speeding past. In a pathetic way we were relieved. Anywhere else and we might not have thought twice about it, but here, not quite sure of our way, in a city that seemed shut into itself, we couldn't help feeling tense. I looked along the street, people were coming and going casually about their business. Only a fire engine.

All the land from Rathfriland to Banbridge along the River Bann is Brontë territory, according to the Northern Ireland Tourist Board brochure. Patrick Brontë recounted his childhood for his children, and from his imaginative descriptions of County Down it is said that the Brontë sisters acquired their material for their novels. Another guide book says "there is hardly prettier, more welcoming countryside in which to get slightly lost."

So we took the "Brontë Homeland Drive" on our way to Belfast. I wonder what the Brontë sisters would think now if they could see the place about which their father so often reminisced. We passed under arches made of wrought iron and about fifteen feet high—"Enniskillen" to the right, "Boyne" to the left, and "No Surrender" in the center—as we drove through Ballyroney looking for the correct road. We finally stumbled upon Drumballyroney Parish Church and School where Patrick Brontë was employed as schoolmaster before entering Cambridge. There is a British flag flying from the steeple and a little notice stating that the church was de-consecrated in 1976.

When we got to the end of the church house road, the main road forked, but there were no further signposts, only a huge red hand—the red hand of Ulster—painted in the center of the street that indicated, for us, whose territory we were really in.

We headed back toward the M1 to Belfast, only slightly reminded of Heathcliff and Cathy by the moors and rolling hills of the Bann Valley.

Mrs. Hazlett's at Ash-Rowan, 12 Windsor Avenue, was our destination in Belfast. On our way to Mrs. Hazlett's, without an adequate map of the city, once again we turned off the motorway at the wrong exit from the roundabout.

Within moments it seemed we were on a road without traffic—an empty street, ominous in itself—heading, as we discovered in panic, toward the Falls Road. "Provo Land" was scrawled in black across the street sign and, in giant lettering, IRA. We pulled over and turned back. Five minutes later we were driving, entirely lost, down a narrow street of small attached houses beneath the fluttering of a dozen red, white, and blue banners. Union Jacks flew from bedroom windows, loyalists slogans were brandished across a bus shelter: "F____ IRA," "IRA Scum." And in front of their hall doors men and women sat, looking out on the street. Waiting. I stopped the car to ask directions of a young-looking man who was walking along the path. I got out beneath the flags in the grip of intimidation, and no sooner had I taken a step toward him than the man tensed. I saw his eyes go past me to the car, a car from the Republic; he stood, half-turned toward me. In one split second he had to decide: stand or run. What was he thinking? Of the others in their doorways watching? Of the amassed flags and banners flying over the little enclave of sectarian hatred, of what watchers might be thinking seeing him here on a street corner talking with a man from the Republic? Informers were shot. At the least, knee-capped.

"Turn left at the end of the street, take the next left, ask anyone then," he said and hurried on. For a hot hour we blundered about Belfast in a series of such narrow, working-class streets feeling the hostile atmosphere and driving in a tense unease past brick buildings painted with Unionist emblems of loyalty, under British flags that seemed to fly to keep strangers out rather than welcome anyone in. How dare we have come to this city at war as tourists, they seemed to say. And when we had driven at last out onto the

Lisburn Road and along to Windsor Avenue, and arrived exhausted at Mrs. Hazlett's door, it was with mixed feelings and a dreadful anxiety at the thought of three more days of the same.

Ash-Rowan is a three-story, red-brick house in one of the quiet elegant avenues on the outskirts of Belfast City. Potted geraniums and summer annuals bloomed around the door-step and across the front of the guest house, and when we rang the bell at the end of our six-hour drive a round-faced, genial woman of fifty came out to greet us with a warm smile.

"Ye were lost? Twice? Oh, no, come in, ye were lost, and och, it doesn't help that they've nicked me sign. Come in."

It was like going inside the home of a favorite, friendly aunt you hadn't seen for some time. She trotted up the stairs ahead of us, talking, passing a huge potted philodendron on the second floor.

"The toilet's there," she said, a little breathlessly, waving a hand at the massive plant and heading up another flight of stairs.

The toilet's *there?* "Sorry?" I said.

"Och, I've been meaning to get that plant trimmed or have something done with it, ye can't even see the door." Mrs. Hazlett chuckled, shook her head, and climbed on. As we followed after her we saw the bathroom door, all but hidden behind the plant. We stopped at the third floor, top of the house, before a door into a shower cabinet, and another next to it into her daughter's old bedroom. And what a lovely room it was! Painted a soft yellow, with a window looking out on the Antrim hills and a church spire, it was furnished with twin deep armchairs, an old-fashioned fireplace dressed for summer with a basket of dried flowers, a big double bed with linen sheets, a big dresser with china teapot and teacups and coffee and teabags and crunchy ginger biscuits, a scattering of books and magazines, and a table and chair for writing. Mrs. Hazlett left us to it after a little speech filled with genuine welcome, and we fell on the bed, safe.

An hour later we were downstairs for dinner. On a table in the deep-pink front room by the window two plates were set for us amid a collection of Victorian antiques.

"Waldorf salad?" asked Mr. Hazlett in a strong northern accent, appearing 'round the door behind us, blue-eyed beneath a crop of silver hair.

We sat at a table that was dappled in sunlight; strains of Mozart emanated from the sitting room across the hall. There was nobody else around. Peace settled over us after the long day. By the time we had been offered and partaken of delicious roast pork on a bed of shallots with mushrooms, and were transferred for our coffee to the sitting room where Bach was now playing, it was impossible not to feel remarkably comfortable and at ease. Mrs. Hazlett, bringing in the coffee, sat herself across the arm of a chair as Chris told her about Deirdre back in Clare.

"I know, I know," she said, "people think it's so dangerous in Belfast, and it's not. Och, it's a lovely city so it is. I think so anyway. What do ye think? I mean people are so frightened to come up. We get so few tourists, mostly businessmen, but it's not the same. We used to have a restaurant. Did ye see the doll in the dining room?"

At this point she paused. Chris said she hadn't seen the doll, so Mrs. Hazlett bounced up from the chair and out. She was back in seconds with an old porcelain doll dressed in the black and white uniform of a Victorian servant girl.

"All the waitresses were dressed like this. But we stopped it. It just became too much for us. In a restaurant you don't really meet people, do you? They're just in and out and you don't get any chance to talk to them. So we opened up four rooms here in Ash-Rowan. We're only open a year. We like to think of it as a rest for friends. What do you think?"

She left us alone after giving us directions for an evening walk, and after coffee and biscuits and Bach we stepped out the front door and down the avenue.

So much of a visit to any place depends upon first impressions. In staying at Bed and Breakfast houses all over the country we had learned that our first welcome colored the impression of the larger place, the city, the village, or the countryside around it. From Mrs. Hazlett's, we walked in the glow of her friendliness. What was her religion, what were her political convictions? We didn't know and they didn't matter to us, just as ours didn't matter to her.

We seemed to be in a relatively wealthy Protestant part of the city. The streets we walked in the evening light were tree-lined and gracious with tall, red-brick houses that glowed redder in the sunset and ran back one after the other to the green mound of Cave Hill. Her father always said Belfast had the most beautiful setting for a city, Mrs. Hazlett had told us. "In a bowl of green hills" was how he'd put it, she said. And it was true. Here along Malone Road, south of the city, every street ended in a view of a hillside. Along this road, leading down past the Ulster Museum to the Botanic Gardens and Queens University, there was an easygoingness, a carefree feeling that one might have expected twenty years before. Young people clustered by a pub. Students abounded, foreign students passed along the sidewalks. People came and went from shops in summer clothes. The world went on normally despite the high-pitched thrumming noise of constantly circling army helicopters. For a moment we were reminded that this was *Belfast,* and looking up at the helicopters Chris said, "It's like being in a goldfish bowl."

It was nine o'clock in the evening. We passed the Ulster Museum with its collections of Irish and international art; Irish furniture, glass, silver, and ceramics; and the gold and silver jewelry recovered from the wreck of the Spanish Armada ship *Girona.* We then turned onto the path between the gates of the Belfast Botanic Gardens and walked down the pathways by beds of marigolds and petunias, lobelia and red salvia. Three men on a bench were talking football in front of the famous 150-year-old glass and wrought-iron Palm House with its dozens of rare tropical plants, many as old as the century. Around the corner, two ladies with walking sticks were resting themselves and talking about the good weather. Their smiles and polite friendly nods encouraged us to bid "good evening" to them. Upon the grass before the Palm House youths had gathered to play cricket. Their calls and cries sounded behind us as we walked around through the rose gardens and along two fledgling perennial flower borders.

Was *this* Belfast then? Was this what it was like here? It was—and it wasn't. For such is the complexity of the tragedy of Northern Ireland that scenes of absolute tranquillity are quite possible and even normal only minutes away from places where the blackened shells of houses, barred gates, and barbed wire bear testament to a state of war.

But in the evening streets around the Botanic Gardens and the university a different world existed in the gilded air. There were no soldiers or flags, armored trucks or sirening squad cars here, only the flowers of the gardens, the surprising smiles and hellos of passersby, tall old trees in summer leaf, the bowl of green hills, and the old-fashioned hump-backed black "London" taxis gliding by.

At Ash-Rowan on Windsor Avenue we slept deeply all night and in the morning came down for Mrs. Hazlett's "Not for the Fainthearted" breakfast fry. It included fried eggs, rashers, sausages, white pudding, black pudding, grilled tomato, fried mushrooms, fried banana, potato bread, and toast. Having stout-heartedly worked my way through most of it while Chris ate a plate of kippers, we sat back sipping coffee and told our hostess how friendly we were finding the city. But like the circling helicopters, all talk in Belfast eventually comes round to "the Troubles."

"Och, it is friendly," she said. "People just don't understand. We all wish it was all over, ye know. But my daughter's twenty now, she's just gone down to the Republic to university, and like, she's never known anything else in Belfast but the troubles. She was born with it on, ye know. And I go in the park sometimes with my grandchildren and I see little wee 'uns, four years old, shaking their fists up at the helicopters. They get it from their parents don't they; it's terrible so it is. But I think you see Belfast *is* friendly, people are lovely despite it all. We can only hope it'll end soon, isn't that it?"

We nodded and listened and later shook her hand and said our goodbyes. Leaving our car at Ash-Rowan for the morning, we walked into the city, down the Dublin Road past the Ulster Hall, down Royal Avenue into the pedestrian shopping heart of Belfast. Until only recently great iron gates barred these streets and shoppers had to pass through checkpoint turnstiles and have their bags and parcels searched. But no more. The gates were wide open and in the bustle of the shopping streets there was all the energy of a living city. However trite it might sound, in every shop we went we encountered in shop assistants and shoppers alike the same friendliness and welcome we had met with at Mrs. Hazlett's. These people cared that we had come to their city. They thanked us across shop counters, hoped we were enjoying our stay and that we would come back. Again and again we came from shops and turned to each other with the same surprise. Was Belfast perhaps the friendliest city in Ireland?

We were going to tour the northern tip of Counties Antrim and Derry today.

"Niall," I said as we were driving, "do you notice anything peculiar about these cars we're passing?"

"No," he answered.

"Then it must be my imagination."

"What are you talking about?"

"Either I'm seeing sunspots, or there are a lot of *red* cars around here."

"What?" He laughed.

"Just watch," I said. "You'll see what I mean in a minute." And sure enough, within seconds, we passed seven cars, six of which were red. Then we got really curious and started to count. There wasn't a single green car that we could see. Yellow, rarely. Orange, well, who drives orange cars anyway? Some white, silver, all shades of blue, but a preponderance of red cars and vans. I would safely estimate that in the extreme northern corner of Northern Ireland every other car is a red car.

"You're right," Niall said. "It's absurd but true."

"It's weird," I said. "Why do you think it is?"

Niall reflected for a moment, scratched his graying beard in mock deliberation, and said almost in a whisper.

"It's the red hand of Ulster again."

And I think he's right. The O'Neill Red Hand is the adopted symbol of Ulster. As the story goes, rivals from an unknown land sailed to Ireland to conquer it. Warriors aboard the ships agreed that whoever touched Irish soil first would become lord. One of the leaders seized the moment by cutting off his left hand and throwing it onto the shore. Who could dispute that he had touched Irish soil first? From this man descended the O'Neills, the royal race of Ulster. The last O'Neill was "Red" Hugh O'Neill, Earl of Tyrone, who escaped to France in 1607 in the famous Flight of the Earls.

I wonder how I would have felt if we had been driving a kelly-green car?

The drive farther north begins at Larne. It takes you up the coast along Sir Charles Lanyon's superbly scenic road laid out in 1837. Today, a surface of smoothest tarmacadam curves in a black ribbon to the Glens of Antrim, the Irish Sea to your right beyond the kind of white seaside railing you might expect in Brighton or Blackpool. "I have seen nothing in Ireland so picturesque as this noble line of coast scenery," Thackeray wrote in 1842 when the road was newly built. It's a touring route par excellence, "reminiscent of the California coast as seen from Highway 1" says Birnbaum's *Ireland.*

The green Mull of Kintyre, Scotland, looms twelve miles out to sea and reminds you of the common links between the two countries, the Gaelic language, the pipes, and, of course, up here in Antrim, the great number of Scots transplanted to Ireland centuries earlier in Elizabeth's misguided effort to supplant the native Irish. At Glenarm begin the nine Glens of Antrim proper: Glenarm, Glencloy, Glengariff, Glenballyeamon, Glenaan, Glencorp, Glendun, Glenshesk, and Glentaisie. They run inland from the coast road, all green hills, woodlands, rivers, and waterfalls. Underneath lies what is said to be a perfect illustration of the geological history of the earth: rock layers of red sandstone, white chalk, basalt, and blue clay. They say people have lived in the Glens for five thousand years. At Cushendall, one of the prettiest villages along the sea route, neolithic ax factories have been found, giving credence to the notion of Ulster's spirit of industry even then, with ax heads being "exported" from here by seafaring warriors from the north.

A few miles farther on we passed Cushendun and climbed the narrowing, winding, and hilly coast road to Torr Head. The cars that had streamed out along the seaside road from Larne were all gone now. A wind blew up here on the balmiest, mildest day in the year and the road was a lonely one. On a tip from Mr. Hazlett, at a National Trust signpost, we turned right driving down a tarred track by thickly wooded slopes that end in the sandy beach of Murlough Bay. Here, in the remotest part of Ulster, with no houses in sight, and cliffs and sheep-dotted hills rising on either side, the tourist is catered to with a good road and well-kept facilities. How English it all seemed to me. For although, thanks to the National Trust, the beauty of the environment is well safeguarded up here, I couldn't help feeling there was a lot to be said for untamed wilderness.

Leaving the scenic coastal road of the Glens of Antrim behind us, we drove through Ballycastle, onto the northern, "Causeway Coast." Ballycastle is home, at the end of August, to the Auld Lammas Fair, which, along with the Puck Fair in Killorglin and the Ballinasloe Horse Fair, is one of the oldest fairs in the country. From Ballycastle we continued to Bushmills, home of the oldest licensed distillery in the world, and, on a day at the end of July, a town festooned with Union Jacks and red, white, and blue banners. This, too, was Northern Ireland.

What was it in such places that sent shivers down my spine? I bear no Ulster Protestant ill will; I blame the sectarian war on the follies of history. In the north of Antrim there are virtually no "Troubles," as such. ("And how could there be?" Chris said. "There are no Catholics. They were driven out.") But in the small towns with big farms of good land around them, this flag-flying, strident loyalism didn't encourage tourism of any kind. We were assaulted with it; there's no friendliness in the air here if you aren't flying the same flag. There must be more flags sold in the six counties of Ulster than in all of England, I thought, and drove on out of Bushmills to our guest house, feeling solemn, unwelcome, and so far from Kiltumper.

Today we had one of those days when everything seems to be slightly askew. It took ages to find our guest house this evening. As there are virtually no B&Bs up here, I was glad that I had booked ahead, but trying to find it by its address was not easy: Black Heath House, Killeague Road, Black-hill, Coleraine. It was six o'clock when we arrived in Coleraine. "Perfect," Niall said. "Just in time for a rest before dinner." "Yes," I said. "But where is Killeague Road or Blackhill?" Two people whom we asked had no idea, so we pulled into a petrol station. The young lad told us that Blackhill was, in fact, six miles out of Coleraine. "Do you know where Garvagh is?" "No." "It's out that way." We followed the signs for Garvagh but no Blackhill. Lost once more, we pulled into another petrol station to discover that Killeague Road was just up ahead, the next right. Finally, we thought. We took the next right, which wasn't Killeague Road, and drove another mile down a lovely road with beautiful soft meadows on either side. "It sure is pretty here," I said. "I'm glad you like it; we may have to sleep in that meadow," Niall said. As it happened, the "eague" had disappeared from the sign and we *were* on the right road, now "Kill" Road, only we were going the wrong way. We had a hard time finding Black Heath House, but we finally arrived just before seven. While we were waiting to be shown to our rooms, I peeked into the breakfast room and glimpsed a cake on a table with white icing and the words "Happy Anniversary." And it was our eighth wedding anniversary.

We were greeted by a friendly enough young man who showed us to our room and quickly disappeared. It was the last we saw of anybody resembling a manager. The room, however, was lovely, with a four-poster bed. Earlier in the day, in Belfast, we had bought swimsuits as there was said to be an indoor pool at this guest house. We looked out the window to see if we could spot the building for the pool, but it was not in view.

Below, in the basement of Black Heath House, we found a restaurant, well known in Coleraine, called MacDuff's. When we were seated at our table I saw a tiny centerpiece of flowers like the kind you see at weddings, with a plastic silver thing stuck on that said "Happy Anniversary." We smiled, amazed and delighted. And all during what proved to be an unfortunate meal—with respect to food and service—I had thought, all will be forgiven if that cake arrives.

But instead of the cake, the dessert menu came. Niall pointed to a table behind us, candlelit with several bowls of flowers on it for a party of eight celebrating their parents' silver anniversary. We left the restaurant a little dismayed but looking forward to a midnight swim. Our search for the pool, however, was fruitless. It either didn't exist or was superbly hidden from the guests.

We left, gladly, in the morning.

As we left Black Heath House and drove back along the Causeway coast a fine mist was blowing in off the sea. We were almost as far from Kiltumper as it was possible to get and still be in Ireland. Giant's Causeway. The name conjures up an image of magical, majestic, grave antiquity. The Giant's Causeway is a series of strange narrow rectangular columns of stone, like steps, marching down into the sea. Weird and mysterious and, whatever your interpretation, an AONB—in British government parlance, an Area of Outstanding Natural Beauty, a perfect example of "Art in Nature." The rocks look like an extraterrestrial landmark on earth, the result of cooled and cracked molten rock 55 million years old.

In Irish mythology, the columns are either the causeway that the giant Finn MacCoul made so his Scotch equivalent, Benandonner, could walk across the sea to begin their fight without the minor fatigue of swimming twelve miles, or the highway he built to his giant ladylove who lived on Staffa, an island in the Hebrides. This last is a romantic interpretation, but the one I liked. In school in Dublin we had all been taught the feats of Finn MacCoul: how he could pluck thorns from his heels while running, how once he had picked up a sod of earth to throw after a fleeing enemy and the sod, landing mid-sea, became the Isle of Man, the hole it left filling with water and becoming Ireland's largest lake, Lough Neagh. Besides all this, Chris and I had a natural penchant for giants. Kiltumper, our own townland, had been named after one, according to one story, and his grave, a mound with a circle of stones, was on the top of the hill at the back of our farm. On his holidays, had our Kiltumper giant walked this way to Scotland?

The Causeway was not "discovered" until the late seventeenth century, when a Bishop of Derry trumpeted the news of its remarkable scenery and a stream of tourists began that hasn't stopped flowing yet. It became obligatory to see it on the Grand Irish Tour. Some, like Richard Pococke in 1754, came to measure it, others, like Susannah Drury, came to make what became famous pictures. It looked like the beginning of the world according to one famous nineteenth-century writer who had to make his way past hordes of begging urchins and guides; a similar experience in the same year caused the German Johannes Kohl to dub it "The Dwarf's Causeway."

Shunning the little tour bus at the top of the hill, Chris and I took the fifteen-minute walk to the strange rock formations, preferring to go guideless into the early morning mist. The narrow black road descends steeply, disappearing into moving shrouds, and as we started down into the crash and fall of an unseen sea, it was impossible not to feel overwhelmed by the eerie atmosphere of the place. Seabirds, fulmars, gulls, and stonechats sounded below us and basalt cliffs towered overhead. Little slides of fallen stones were stopped midway between the clifftops and the water and from their fallen stillness, their perpetual balance, emanated the sense of frozen time that was the mood of the Causeway. Sleeping giant's breath, said Chris, meaning the mist that was folding and parting thickly around us, opening views down the road to the shore. In the distance a man with a black beret and a stick moved before us. From somewhere behind came the sound of children's voices.

By the time we reached the "honeycomb" (the Middle Causeway), with its yellow-and-black-colored lichen strongly marked, we found ourselves inside a landscape that had slowly changed as we walked through it. At first only bits of rock like rounded squares emerged. Then they began to grow and multiply, one on top of the other. Stacks of them. Weird, lunar, and regular; a triangle made of hundreds of hexagonal stones rising tightly together, like pipes, going out into the sea. It was Aird Snout headland. Past it, farther along the coast, are numerous and equally strange formations: the Wishing Well, The Giant's Granny, The King and His Nobles. Each one is an extraordinary sculpture of nature.

We climbed out on the little salt-sprayed peninsula of Aird's Snout, pointing toward Scotland. The sea rushed in past us. The black headland at our backs softened under a veil of mist and we sat down in that remarkable place where the surfaces of half of the stones were nicely shaped for the behinds of the seagazers but were in fact the "ball and socket" joints of fractured columns of varying heights that jutted out to sea. Here, wrapped in sea mist and bird cries, was a place that imprinted itself upon you. It was human-diminishing, dwarfing. Nature was the Giant, and upon these stones of her causeway we sat, hushed, and stared at the mysteriousness of the world.

· Chapter Nine ·

*Conversation about a cuckoo—Afternoon tea—We lose
a tenner at the Galway Races—On to West Mayo—
A goat is crowned*

Again and again, as a stream of summer visitors have come
calling at our house, we have heard the same thing: Yes, the
landscape of the country was more beautiful and varied than
many expected, the mountains more dramatic and lonely,
the white-sand seashores more lovely, but more important,
it was the people living in the landscape who made Ireland
special. No visitor left without saying so in one way or
another. And for many of them it was the chance
encounter—the knock on the farmer's door for directions
that turned into an all-afternoon visit, the woman who

came out with floury hands and discovered herself a cousin—that made the whole country come alive and the holiday memorable. Its people are the unmapped attractions of Ireland.

This evening, sitting at the round table by the kitchen window and looking out down the garden, I saw a priest from a neighboring parish come strolling up our path. Chris had gone out and Deirdre was asleep. As I opened the door the smiling, blue-eyed man began to utter a fast-flowing stream of words.

"Niall, good evening. Do you know what I'm going to tell you now? You don't, you see. But I was in Dublin recently and I was reading your book and I came across that little verse Mary Donnellan gave you about the cuckoo, and you know that isn't the way we learned it at all when we were going to school. No.

> The Cuckoo comes in April
> He sings his song in May
> In the middle of June
> He whistles his tune and
> In July he flies away.

"That's what she gave you. But we had it differently, you see, and I'll tell you why now shortly and maybe it'll make sense to you. You see what we had was:

> The Cuckoo comes in April
> He sings his song in May
> In the middle of June
> *He changes his tune* and
> In July he flies away.

"And now, you see, Niall, I used to wonder about that word 'changes' there, he changes his tune, and what did it mean. Was it a change in attitude to life or what was it. Well now, I'll tell you. You see a priest friend of mine recently told me he had opportunity to hear a cuckoo close up singing his song. He was driving along doing a bit of shooting out the window of his car, do you see, and didn't he stop and hear the cuckoo right next to him a few feet away. And now Niall, what he told me was this: To you and me the song of the cuckoo sounds 'cuck-ooo, cuck-ooo' like that. But this man said it was more like 'cuck-oo-whist, cuck-oo-whist.' With this 'whist' business at the end you see, only you and I don't normally hear that part because it doesn't carry, the 'cuck-oo-whist.' So back to Mary Donnellan, you see I was wondering over this and was thinking maybe that was it, do you get me, that 'whist' that she meant when she said 'whistles his tune,' do you see? A kind of a whist of a whistle, like that. Or, if you've ever had opportunity to hear a cuckoo in June, Niall, you'll notice it isn't at all like the song he sings in May. Did you ever notice, Niall? You didn't I suppose. Well now, one day you will. You see, it's more a kind of 'cuck-hoo,' low down in his throat, 'cuck-hoo,' like the battery going low or something, you know? 'Cuck-hoo.' That's it, yes, 'cuck-hoo.'

"Well, anyways, I have an article here now, let me see, yes, here it is, on the cuckoo. All about him and his ways. There you are now, you can keep that, I have copies of it. Well, in the name of God is that the time? No, I won't stay. Say hello to Crissie for me. I'll see you again. God Bless."

A funny thing happened today while we were sitting having our tea. There came a knock at the front door. Niall went to answer it and outside standing in the drizzle was an American lady.

"Hello," she said.

"Hello," said Niall. He has grown quite used to the forthright American way, and to greeting unexpected visitors, and he anticipated her next words. But this woman hesitated, seemingly puzzled by Niall's face, before asking earnestly, "Do you serve afternoon tea?"

Well, we've come to expect many things now from our friendly and curious visitors, and we have met with some unusual requests, but this one quite dumbfounded Niall.

"No," he answered in a kind of quizzical West Clare melodic note with a long o-sound that rises into the air.

"But I saw the sign," she said, staring hard at Niall's bemused face.

"Sign? What sign?" he asked turning his back to her a moment and peeking his head in the door to where I was holding in my giggles, with difficulty.

"The sign at the bottom of the path." She pointed beyond our garden gate to where, it suddenly dawned on both of us, stands, crookedly, our mailbox, made out of a biscuit tin bearing the manufacturer's brand name: "Afternoon Tea."

"Yes. I mean no," responded Niall, "that's for our biscuits, I mean, our post. That's where our letters go. That's our mailbox!"

"Oh," she said nonplussed. "Well, I'm really looking for the home of Niall Williams and Christine Breen. Do you know them?"

One morning when we woke rain was falling. It had come in overnight, a fine thin mist of falling gray that made the hills of Tumper vanish behind us and hid the valley beyond the front garden. A silent pale wetness overlay the countryside, and in its persistence the three long months of blue summer began to fade. The hill fields, summer browned for the first time in years, began to slowly green once more. I wore Wellingtons and pull-ups going out through them. The drain that followed the hill down by the roadside ran like a stream again and the cows all clustered under the sheltering blackthorn hedge in the evenings. After a string of misted, soft rainy days, the wind off the west began to pick up. Little squally showers blew. The tall purple spires of larkspur thrashed along the garden path, the eight-foot-high fuchsia began to go off bloom and dead leaves began to gather at the back door. There was no cold in the wind though, and the memories of summer still warmed us. It was still August, a season of fairs and festivals in Ireland, of the Galway Races and the Puck Fair among others. And so one rainy evening Chris unfolded our now crisscrossed and worn map of the country and ran her finger into Connemara.

The following noon we arrived in Galway in the drizzle. At the roundabout on the outskirts of our favorite city, a hand-made, makeshift sign said "Races." In a moment we were in heavy traffic and Chris took out the paper "to study form." Neither of us knew anything about horseracing—little enough about horses for that matter—and reading the *Irish Times* guide to the afternoon's races was no great help either. It was names that appealed to us rather than facts like records, riders, or trainers.

" 'I'm Confident,'" Chris read out, " 'trainer N. McDonagh. Innocent Choice, P. Mullins . . .'" These two we fancied, and would put our tenner on one of them in the afternoon's big race.

For a pound a farmer's field was the unofficial carpark, and through a gap in a stone wall and along by the track we made our way to the entrance. In the light rain men in blue and gray suits ushered women in bright dresses through the turnstiles where a small boy in an anorak played his tin whistle for change. Inside, hundreds of little murmurous gatherings of people were standing around, drinks and form sheets in hand, the mood light and easy. This was Ladies Day at the Galway Races, and through the crowds, moving from the grandstand to the parading circle, from the bookies on their tea chests to the company and club tents for drinks and sandwiches, there was every color and style of dress. Oblivious to the drizzle, a long-legged and tanned girl in a short marigold dress and straw hat paraded past.

There were two women in blue hats and white gloves; another in a striking emerald-green jacket and short, straight black skirt; one all feathers and tropical; her friend in scarlet with a dress that reached the ground; a refined-looking lady of sixty under a blue parasol; a pair of debutantes with their mother, all correct and proper; a dark-haired girl in a white dress that seemed to have been through a shredder; an entire parade of brightly dressed ladies passing through the crowd. Hats galore. Friends came to meet friends, to see what they had come up with to wear this year. It was a social spectacle. There was Father so-and-so with his binoculars and his cap, there was John; "What have you got in the next one, John? How did you do yesterday? Oh, don't talk to me about that British nag. What are you drinking?" And on and on the drink and chat flowed. Fresh and battered £10, £20, and £50 notes were handed over. Glasses of porter were downed as the Guinness Jazz Band played bravely against the rain. In a kind of perfected Galway-races-rhythm the grandstands emptied and the bars and tents filled moments after each race.

As Chris and I trailed the crowd that was dispersing "for momentary liquid sustenance," as one man described it, over the public address came an announcement: "The competition for Best Dressed Lady is currently taking place behind the Corrib grandstand." There, the judges were scanning the crowd. The ladies stood around and chatted and laughed. Few of them appeared to be thinking of the two £500 prizes on offer, or to be concerned about the light rain falling on them. I had stopped to make a note upon a notepad when I noticed a cluster of ladies gathering in front of me, moving very slowly past, and then, in moments, sauntering back again, high heels stepping carefully over the puddled ground. Realizing I was being mistaken for a judge, I hastened with Chris back up into the stand.

Half an hour later in the Galway Guinness Hurdle, I'm Confident, the horse we meant to bet on, wanted to bet on, should have bet on, passed four fallers at the final fence to come sailing home at 33–1. The horse we *had* bet on, Innocent Choice, turned out to be a nonrunner!

As the punters filed out of the stand and down to the bar we made our way out of the grounds in the rain, past two ladies in long dresses hurrying, late, and on into Galway City.

"Psychologically," I said to Chris, "we won that race."

She let out a groan. "Thirty-three to one!" was what she said.

In the rain-gray light I don't know of any other city in Ireland that looks as nice as Galway, with its colorful wooden shopfronts and gray Galway stone, with its canals and narrow streets, with the Druid Theatre and the Galway Arts Festival, with its specialty shops and craft shops and its art and traditional culture. There's the very purple shopfront of Dympna Byrne's store, the red of Cobwebs, a nostalgia shop, and the deep blue Quay. And then there's

Kenny's, green, with hanging baskets and paintings and books in the windows. Those are the colors of Galway.

For us, a trip to Galway is never complete without a trip to Kenny's Bookshop and Art Gallery. Today was no exception. We ate at Cross Street and wound our way down High Street to Kenny's. We usually browse for an hour or so, looking at new titles and new artwork and the current exhibition in the gallery. We have been told that they stock our two books; to see our books displayed in Kenny's would be a sort of crowning thrill.

I went straight to the gallery and children's book section while Niall stayed in the front with the books of Irish interest. He was browsing over Kavanagh's *Green Fool* when I came back to him. I had given up urging Niall to ask about either of our books when quite unexpectedly he went up to the counter and said to one of the Kenny brothers, "I believe you have sold a book of ours. It's called *O Come Ye Back . . .*" began Niall when Mr. Kenny exclaimed, "*to Ireland!*" He quickly offered his hand and Niall introduced us. Mrs. Kenny, overhearing, came over and shook hands, too. She said she especially liked our second book.

"I was reading it at five in the morning," she said, "and I nearly fell out of bed when I saw the part about Kenny's. And I do remember when you came in here asking about a dehumidifier around Christmas time." While she was talking, her son went off and when he returned he was carrying the Guest Book. He showed us where Austin Clarke and Liam O'Flaherty had signed and I spotted Peter O'Toole's signature. We proudly added our signatures and talked about the books and our current project.

Then, not one to miss an opportunity, I asked them what they thought of the paintings on the jacket covers.

"Yes, they're quite good, in fact, you should talk to my brother Tom. He organizes the art exhibitions."

An encouraging word from Kenny's. This meant so much to me.

For almost ten years now, Michael Viney's weekly column, "Another Life," in the Saturday *Irish Times* has been an inspiration to us. I can remember reading it during the days of our courtship in Dublin, searching out each week the few hundred words and pen-and-ink sketch that brought to life the world of a man who had left a career and moved to the west, to Mayo. In New York two years later, my father would mail me week-old copies of the Saturday newspaper, and there, sitting on a commuter train going to Manhattan, or spending a quiet lunchtime in the office reading "Another Life," I caught the infectious dream of a life on the land in the west of Ireland. On New Year's Eve of last year, Chris sat in the kitchen and, spreading the paper to read "Another Life," discovered it was about a Chris and Niall who had moved from America and lived in a small West Clare townland called Kiltumper.

Now, eight months later, leaving Galway City and winding northwest through Connemara under a cloud-embattled sky, we were driving to visit Michael Viney.

At Oughterard, in the pretty village by Lough Corrib, loved by two centuries of sporting fishermen and known as the gateway to Connemara, the rain began to sweep down. With turfsmoke rising, it was easy to imagine nineteenth-century travelers holed up for days in hotels here with strong tea and stronger whiskey, waiting out the stormy weather before leaving for the bleak beautiful roads into the mountains. Beyond this town, they had read, was a wild, sparsely inhabited landscape through which a brown wind blew down off gray mountains, across blue lakes and black bog. Connemara and Mayo: the romantic music of their names, the song-like quality, mocked what was absolute silence when you stopped on the road and stood in a mountain valley, listening to nothing at all. Out there, beyond Oughterard, in the land between Lough Corrib and the sea were what many believed were the descendants of the *true* Irish, those driven west by Cromwell, old Connacht clans who lived on out there on the worst land of the island, along with Aran its most truly Gaelic part, and for many its most beautiful.

Oughterard is now one of the most popular fishing centers in Ireland. The Germans and the English in particular cluster here with rods and nets, buying flies and walking through the town in rubber boots and bright rain gear, making me think all the more of the desolate Connacht wilderness beyond the town. For almost a year now Irish fishermen have been in dispute with the government over the introduction of a new fishing license. Entering and leaving Oughterard there were half a dozen banners and hand-painted signposts proclaiming "No Fishing Rod License," and "Boycott Here." A trace of the resolute independence of the west, I thought, as we gazed out through the rain and drove along the winding road out of town and on toward the Maamturk Mountains.

Turf banks like black wounds in the brown bog slit the landscape. Yellow and green plastic fertilizer bags full of sods lay piled near the roadside, reeks were stacked darkly against gray sky. To say the scene was magical, spell-like, extraordinary, said nothing of what it was like at all. Whole mountains seemed to appear and disappear again before our eyes, coming and going like walking giants through the mists of rain. The swiftness of changing clouds, the breaks of light, the sudden gold fringe behind blackblue clouds transformed the view even as we watched it. No photograph could ever catch it, for the essence of it *was* change, wind bringing clouds across mountaintops and turning blues to purples and greens to all shades of brown. The landscape wove itself around us as we drove slowly through it. As the rain eased, we saw the peaks of the Twelve Pins in the distance. There were few houses anywhere. It seemed to be raining hard only two hundred yards away from where we were. Views closed and opened even as we looked.

From Maam Cross we took the road for Leenane, a favorite place for us in Ireland. At the bottom of a road through the great wet loneliness that is Connemara, you come to Leenane and the sea. Here, nestled fjord-like between a row of high green sloping mountains, is Killary harbor. Bicycles and cars were parked along the waterfront by the tea shop. The rain lifted, and the brightening light over Killary made Leenane seem a haven.

We drove around the far side of the harbor and headed north between Ben Gorm and Mweelrea mountains. As we swept past Lough Doo and the Delphi fisheries, as the mountains rose up on either side of us, the landscape kept stopping me. I wanted to get out and walk. For all the hardness of gray rock and stoney ground, for all the weathered bleakness of every view, there was something utterly, eternally soft and welcoming in the misting rains that fell there. I wanted to stop, wander silently out across soggy boggy places, over rock-strewn slopes, and up and out of sight, vanishing into mountain mist among the sheep. Up in Murrisk somewhere, that's where I'd go, hearing in that name both the strong vowel and burr of mountain wind and the soft *ish* of the rain. But Michael and Ethna Viney had invited us for lunch. Our appointment with the Vineys drew us on. We took a left-hand turn, down a narrow boreen for several bumping miles, and again out of the mountains to the sea, a sweep of white sand and an empty beach, and then down the road to the house. As I stopped the car Michael Viney came out to greet us. A silver-brown-haired, fit-looking man in a blue sweater, he shook our hands and welcomed us. As we stepped inside to the book-lined sitting room overlooking the garden and the spectacular waves breaking on the shore, I looked at Chris and she smiled. We had arrived at another of the places of our dream's beginning.

Our visit to the Vineys' was a dream fulfilled all right. They let us in on a secret. The secret is one word: compost. If I ever had my doubts about the benefits, no, the miracles, of compost, they have been fully put to rest now after seeing the Vineys' garden. It's hard to believe, but they are almost entirely self-sufficient on one acre. And they do it completely without pesticides. Ethna's luncheon included five different salads made entirely from her summer produce. Zucchini and basil was Niall's favorite. Michael explained his method of gardening in the sea-windy climate of his little corner of Mayo while he was bringing us around.

"We grow extra." This means, I guessed, extra for the pests and the wind, then Nature, in her bountifulness, leaves enough for the Vineys.

When they first started gardening twelve years ago, Michael had stuck some fuchsia twigs in the earth to support the beans as they grew. At that time they had no protection from the wind. By the summer's end he discovered quite delightedly that they had taken root. Now the garden is literally a maze of neatly trimmed fuchsia hedges with vegetable beds tucked safely here and there. In winter the hedge is a thicket of networking branches and twigs because it is kept so closely cropped in summer. It gives a little in the wind but bounces back. At the moment he is very proud of a rose garden he has started.

In their garden they had some plants that I had never heard of, like an edible Japanese chrysanthemum. They had an asparagus bed, globe artichokes, and a ten-foot-long patch of Jerusalem artichokes that made a fine summer hedge.

Michael said he liked weeds and let them grow in corners. There were no concrete paths or stone steps, just grass walkways and clover, a bed of comfrey, a tiny "orchard," tomatoes growing in a lean-to glass house, and the scent of lemon balm as we brushed past and rounded a corner into yet another garden compartment. Now and then I lifted my eyes to the white strand just four miles below and imagined gardening here with the Atlantic Ocean to sing to. It was a little piece of heaven fallen from the sky.

Thinking of the lace-patterned leaves on my own cabbages and Brussels sprouts I asked how they controlled the cabbage butterfly and her caterpillars. A healthy dose of good old phosphate-free soap and water was the answer. In fact, there seemed to be no sign of any pests. The plants were so healthy and strong that either there was enough for everybody to eat or the plants simply withstood the occasional invasion, whereas my plants raise the white flag, keel over, and surrender. His red cabbages were nearly three feet in diameter! His Brussel sprouts four feet high!

Michael throws everything in the compost heap. None of this worrying about insufficient heat buildup to kill seed heads. Everything that grows out, goes in. At the moment, two huge piles of yellow ragwort, with its pretty daisy-like heads, poisonous to the Vineys' white pony in the next field, lay like discarded bouquets, waiting their turn at the compost bin.

"If you bury it, like I do, then you don't have to worry about weed seeds germinating," he said and there was just a touch of playfulness in his voice. He made it sound so easy. I can only hope that in a few more years, when my garden is more established, when the balance of pests and their predators are even, which is supposed to happen after chemicals are eliminated from the garden, and when we are more self-sufficient, I can invite the Vineys to a summer luncheon and show them around *my* garden. And I will let them admire *my* compost heap.

Our goat is a lucky goat. She arrived, wild out of the hills, at the back of our house one morning, and never left. She adopted our little herd of cows and calves, and we had come to believe it was true when our neighbors told us she could be the bearer of good luck. It was shortly after her arrival in Kiltumper that we had been approved for adoption and been able to bring Deirdre into our lives. The goat was lucky, there was no denying it, and no separating her from us either. If I moved the cows from one field to another the goat hung back, watched, and waited. She wouldn't come through the open gateway. Instead she stood until I had reshut the gate and then she jumped the stonewall and trotted in among the cows. When we herded the cows down to the cabins for tests or doses, the goat came, too. She had attached herself with fierce loyalty to our little farm, and we would not want to drive our good luck away.

When we heard that the Puck Fair, one of the ancient fairs of Ireland, was built around the coronation of the finest male goat in County Kerry and his reign over the town for three days and nights, we couldn't help but want to see it.

A mile from Killorglin the traffic came to a stop. In fields and gaps, at gateways and roadsides, cars were pulled over, and a steady stream of men, women, and children marched down the road toward the town. Now and then, a man coming from the fair and leading a horse or pony walked against the crowd. All eyes measured the beast and passed on. From the bridge across the River Laune, the steep hill of the town's main street was alive with people. Since early morning the vans of Ireland's Travellers (tinkers) had been steadily arriving and opening their stalls, offering everything from radios and clocks to wickerwork baskets, newfangled potato peelers, sets of spanners, plastic dolls, and pop guns. Others had set up a well-worn roulette wheel, a shooting range, a hoop-toss, and a fortune-telling tent. They lined the street on either side, quoting bargain prices, giveaway offers—"£5-the-lot"—to the moving onlookers and went in and out of their vans to throw more new merchandise onto their stalls.

Along the side street by the church railings a horse fair was in full swing. Under a drizzling sky men in caps and a few women moved in clusters around seventy or so animals—horses, ponies, and donkeys. Every class of horse-flesh was here, from hairless bow-backed old mules to miniature toy-like little horses no bigger than a tall dog; from great hefty gray mares and a few fine-looking hunters to the brown-and-white-spotted pinto ponies of the Travellers. Tethered to anything that could be found—the church gates, the lampposts, small trees, the backs of vans, or simply held in the street at the end of a rope—the animals attracted small crowds, and in each crowd was the mumbled half-talk and haggling of dealing. Men coughed prices into their hands, spat, looked away, sniffled, shook their heads, tipped their caps, scratched the small hairs of their ears, smacked their hands on the backs and bums of horses. As the street air filled with the thick smell of brown-gold horse dung, the real business of the fair went on. Our neighbor Martin had joined us for the two-day jaunt to the fair. With

Martin counseling us on the quality of the animals, we moved back and forth through them in the rain. I watched two men trying to make a bargain. Neither was entirely sober, and the buyer's offer was still £50 short of the seller's price. Their voices grew louder and they swayed beside the horse. Then, a small teenage Traveller grabbed each of them by the wrist. Standing between them, he held their hands almost touching in the air and uttered a stream of numbers and encouragement until they gruffly agreed. He spat and joined them in a handshake. The horse was sold, and from a coat pocket more than £1,000 in damp curling £10 notes was handed over. The men walked off toward the pubs together leaving the boy, smiling, with the animal. Up and down the streets we walked in and out among horses and men, weighing up, listening, watching, gauging prices and sellers. So much went on before a figure was mentioned. There was a whole production before negotiations began: an approach, a shaking of the head, a drifting away, a coming back later, some minor criticism, an entirely disinterested question, Is she quiet? or something like it, with a casual unimpressed, Is that right? following the answer. It was all part of an unwritten code of behavior that went back to the ancient fairs of Ireland. "Whatever would they think," whispered Chris, "if we walked right up and said, outright, a thousand pounds?"

All afternoon the crowds gathered. At the beginning of the hill street a band of young pipers from Fermoy stood still behind the tricolor and played. Farther up, two men with a guitar and accordion sang "The Fields of Athenry," and ten yards away a group of stout drinkers, pint glasses in hand, were roaring themselves red in the face with a rendition of

"The Town I Loved So Well." The rain held off in the gray-green Slieve Mish Mountains to the north, and the Macgillacuddy Reeks to the south, as more and more people made their way through the standstill traffic up the street to the as yet empty wooden tower in the square, as horse-dealers left the fair for the pubs, as tempers heated a little, and the air grew tangled with smells of frying chips, stale urine, porter, and horse dung. Killorglin was almost ready for the annual Puck Fair.

At our position before the wooden tower at the top of the square, we waited in the jostling crowd for the official opening. Here, any moment, at the end of a parade through the streets of the town would come the finest wild male goat. He would be brought up onto the lower platform of the tower and crowned by the Queen of the Fair, a twelve-year-old girl. Then, hoisted fifty-two feet to the top of the tower, he would "reign" as King Puck, overseeing three days of festivity and drinking—Gathering Day, Reaping Day, and·Scattering Day—until he was brought down and released in the Kerry Mountains. From the Puck Fair program, Chris read to us scraps of the fair's history.

" 'It is generally regarded by historians,' " she read, " 'that Puck Fair is the oldest annual fair in existence. . . . Some historians claim that the festival may have been a pre-Christian celebration. . . . History shows us that the most unlikely characters can and have become monarchs in their time, but surely none more unlikely than King Puck. . . . Every town in Ireland will boast that its festival is unique. But what makes Puck different from most other festivals is its sense of History, its friendliness and its humor. It has always been a major tourist attraction, but it has refused to cast off its earthy roots and become a gimmick.'"

At the lower platform of the tower a Kerry man in a dress suit and bow tie took the microphone and announced the beginning of the parade. In the close crowd we could see nothing, but the familiar swirling sounds of pipers and drums gradually rose up the hill street. Young boys and girls climbed out of upstairs windows and sat on ledges to watch, others drew aside curtains and craned their necks round the corner. Where was the goat? Where was Puck? Heretofore, the goat had always been captured in the nearby Macgillacuddy Reeks, Ireland's highest mountains. But this year, in a gesture of goodwill to its sister fair, the Auld Lammas in Antrim, a goat had been captured at Fair Head and flown to the County Kerry airport and from there brought to Killorglin to be crowned.

The parade passed before us as we craned to see. After the tops of the heads of the local Irish Countrywomen's Association ladies, the haircuts of the members of the youth club, the nearly invisible members of the credit union, came the goat himself, standing high on a crate in full view, draped in a purple cloak and tied at his four legs to the corners of his stand. There was applause. He was white and long-bearded with a curling horn span of two feet. As he passed over the heads of the crowd to the platform where young Queen Cliona Foley was waiting to crown him, we couldn't help being struck by the strangeness of it all. There was a pagan quality to it all right, a fertility rite at harvest-time. On the one hand, it felt weirdly ancient to be standing in a crowded town square waiting to see a goat crowned, and on the other, completely ridiculous.

As the moment came for Queen Cliona to crown the

goat, a battery of photographers appeared and blocked the crowd's view. We caught a flash of gold, a glimpse of the goat's head. Then, the pulling action of men at ropes, and there, jerkily, swaying, rose King Puck on his stand, through an opening on the second floor, and up, to reign for three days over the town and citizens of Killorglin.

· Chapter Ten ·

*From Kiltumper to Donegal—The magic of
Glencolumbkille—Trá—Home again, home again,
jiggedy jig*

"O Danny Boy, the pipes, the pipes are calling, From
glen to glen, and down the mountainside, The summer's gone and all the rose is falling . . ."

Of all songs, this one has a kind of everlasting and beautiful
melancholy that, despite what popularity has done to it
through a million maudlin or drunken renditions, has kept
its impact. Ten years ago, three weeks an emigrant, during
a hot humid New York summer I heard Chris's brother Joe,

then a voice major at Juilliard, sing it in the living room of their mother's house in Westchester. He sang his soul into it, with shut eyes and shaking fingertips, sang it over the hot still air, the burnt brown grass, the crickets, and the drone of the highway, until for each of us listening there were only cool mists and sweeping mountainsides, the impossibly sad green glens of a half-imagined Ireland. "O Danny Boy." I never forgot the power of that moment, the sadness and longing that had overwhelmed me. I was literally transported. To where? To what Ireland? To a place I didn't actually see until five years later. Then, on holiday from our jobs in New York, touring with Chris through the mountains in Donegal, we had come upon a place of such special beauty that in some inner part of us we recognized it. Yes, there, that's the Ireland we had imagined: Glencolumbkille.

We had saved it all year, planning it ahead of us the way children plan treats. After everywhere else, at the end of summer, before settling in to the turf fires of Kiltumper for the winter, we would hole up for a week in Glencolumbkille. Before the calves had to be weaned from the cows and the first bales of hay to be thrown over the back wall, before we brought in turkeys to be reared for Christmas, before those nights when we would have to load up the range with turf before going to bed, we packed the car one morning, secured the bicycles on the roof rack, and set off for Donegal.

We left at first light and drove through the cold gray emptiness of the countryside in a hush. Places slipped past. Towns were fast asleep. Beyond Gort a line of Travellers' caravans were parked outside the entrance to Lady Gregory's Coole Park, the one-time center of the Irish literary revival. The mansion was a ruin now, pulled down in 1941 for its stone. But on the grounds the "autograph tree" still stood, carved with the initials of W. B. and J. B. Yeats, Shaw, Synge, O'Casey, and others. Farther along the main road to Galway was the turn for Yeats's tower at Thoor Ballylee. We had gone there in January on the fiftieth anniversary of the poet's death, and walked about in the damp loneliness of the place. As we drove past I remembered a whole catalog of impressions: forty-three beech trees and in the winter muddiness a breath of marsh marigolds outside, the sound of water running ceaselessly as the little river swept past the gray stone tower, the ivy-covered specters of lightning-struck trees, the cold air in the winding stair, the dampness, the weeping feel of the stone, the narrow, heavy, and mattressless wooden bed—a place "for my old age" wrote Yeats—shocking me a little with its austerity. Then we went up the curve of steps and through a low arched door out to warm air and the battlements, "the warmest room in the house," with far views of Gort fields and a roof of gray Galway sky.

We passed Galway and drove into Mayo. By now, Deirdre, fully awake in the backseat, had taken to the idea of these sleeping towns, and as we passed through them she joyfully shouted, "Wake up you lazybones!" It was just nine o'clock and, on a Saturday morning, Mayo people were still abed. Only in Knock was there sign of life, with lines of cars and early morning pilgrims going to Mass and visiting the shrine. At any time, on any day of the year, there would be people there.

Above Mayo we drove into Sligo town for mid-morning breakfast. Showers of rain whipped down, and coming from a break in their morning session, students and teachers from the two-week Yeats's Summer School crowded into the cafe. Sligo was Yeats country proper, the special places of his childhood were here, and place names that rang out of much of his poetry were the signposts at crossroads. Minutes beyond the town, in the churchyard at Drumcliff, under the cloud-hid top of Ben Bulben Mountain, was his grave. Over tea and biscuits, we saw conclaves of his admirers of a dozen nationalities. The immaturity of the early phase was proclaimed by a Japanese, a German lauded the merits of the "Tower" poems. For a Texan, there was nothing but the "Later" poems. I imagined old Willie, happy in Sligo, as we hurried back to the car and on toward Donegal.

Through a torrential downpour we glimpsed the sign reading "Welcome to County Leitrim" and nothing more until, windscreen wipers going at full speed, we glimpsed another sign welcoming us to County Donegal. In the drenched seaside streets of Bundoran the weather lifted. A glimmer of brightness after the downpour made the road shine, and children, on the last days of their holidays, started to come out again. Bundoran was touched with the nostalgic air of Irish seaside towns in winter, with gray seas crashing just in front of a line of old brightly colored guest houses. There was the vaguely desperate air of rainy holidays, with untouched bunches of plastic buckets and spades blowing on hooks outside grocery shops. Postcard stands had been brought inside the door, out of the rain. I felt anxious about the weather and wondered how we'd manage in Glencolumbkille.

Finally, after five hours, we reached Donegal town. In its "Diamond," the square, stands a monument to "the Four Masters" — Michael O'Cleary, Fearfeasa O'Maolconry,

Peregrine O'Duigenan, and Peregrine O'Cleary—who, between 1632 and 1636 composed their *Annals,* covering the history of the world up to 1616.

At the Diamond we turned left on the road to Killybegs, past Mountcharles and Dunkineely, and then on toward Kilcar. The signposts were now in Irish. It was midday, and the combination of our early morning exodus from Clare and the narrowing, winding Donegal roads began to infuse the journey with a sense of endlessness. The landscape became less and less populated. We were moving between the sea and bog, with purplish brown mountains rising into clouds. Wind was shaking the bikes on the roof rack, clouds traveled smooth and fast along mountainsides, and you could see rain falling not a quarter of a mile away. For miles there was not a house to be seen. Mist came down to the roadsides and made the white dots of sheep disappear. At the little village of Carrick, the last before Glencolumbkille, we stopped for groceries, and then drove on down the continuous softly rising and falling wave of the road. There were turfbanks cut on either side of us, reeks of stacked turf black with rain, or mounded white and green because of the big plastic fertilizer bags into which the turf had been gathered—the only sign of man in a deserted landscape. From the lower slopes of Slieve League Mountain came rushing waters, browned with bog, curving into streams, and emptying into the ocean.

We came to a signpost that told us Glencolumbkille was six miles in one direction, three miles in the other. We took the three-mile route and saw the sea in minutes. On a small hill overlooking the water and Rathlin O'Birne Island off the shore was the house where we would be staying, "my holiday home," as Deirdre called it. A white bungalow, a one-story, three-bedroomed house with kitchen, bathroom, and sitting room with a fireplace, two armchairs, and a couch. On one side its windows opened onto views of Malin Bay and the nearby island. Simple and small with white pictureless walls and a worn fawn-colored carpet, it was comfortable.

Within half an hour we had unpacked and were on our bicycles, pedaling into the small village of Glencolumbkille. A strong Atlantic wind was gusting. The narrow road curved away from under the shadow of a brown mountain and along by stretches of moorgrass and heather. We seemed to be bicycling inland, the sea at our backs and nothing but the mountains and silvered rainwater rushing through gulleys in the bogs around us. As we rounded a bend in the road— perhaps our favorite bend in all of Ireland—there before us was the sea once more and a greeny blueness crashing with high spray into the jagged Icelandic-looking cliffside of Glen Head. It was exhilarating and surprising. It was like traversing a little personal island, coming from the sea around the mountain to the sea again all within the space of two miles or so. No matter how often we saw it in the days ahead, each time we experienced the same thrill as we came around that bend. At my back, a contented Deirdre began to murmur and point and exclaim from her bike seat: "Oh, it's lovey!" She was right. It was. We paused a minute and looked out over the hillside falling sharply below us and across to Glen Head. We cycled on and sat back for a curving freewheel down into Glencolumbkille.

·   ·   ·

The village itself is tiny: a church, two grocery shops, a petrol pump, a post office, and a knitwear shop that doubles in summer as a tourist office with a little grill-room restaurant above it. Around the village, dotted on the lower slopes of the encircling mountains, are a number of houses, some thatched, with a potter's shop, a marine painting gallery and another shop for tweeds and knitwear. A mile or so outside the village, facing a small horseshoe-shaped beach, are a number of thatched cottages closely grouped together and comprising the "Folk Village."

"I love this place," Chris said. "I know this will sound corny, but I keep expecting us to disappear into the mist like the two Yanks in *Brigadoon*. This is one of the most special places in Ireland."

With the rain about to pour down on us we turned and started back for our house, this time cycling into the ferocious wind that brought tears to our eyes. That evening, with Deirdre sleeping in her "holiday bed," Chris and I enjoyed the warmth of a glowing turf fire as we looked out to the sea and the low, flat whale-back of the island. The last patches of pale sky were quickly vanishing into great sweeps of broken night-cloud. At the small Ostan, or hotel, at Malinmore, I could see two children on swings, playing in the Atlantic breeze. Past them, sloping fields led down to the land's end. The children rose and fell happily on the swings, as the night darkened and the red flicker of the lighthouse on Rathlin O'Birne flashed its warnings to the sea. Chris looked up from the book she was reading. "Imagine a childhood *here*," she said.

We are in the throws of toilet-training, and toilet-training while traveling presents its own highlights. Deirdre, invariably, decides she has to "go" while we're in the car. She thinks it's special to "go" on the road, and once outside she doesn't always want to return to the backseat. Sometimes she doesn't have to "go" at all. Today, on the way back from a short drive, Deirdre made her request. Niall pulled over straightaway and we got out. As we prepared to undress her she spotted a pony in the field across the road. Suddenly she no longer had to "go." Instead she was across the road in a flash saying, "Mommy, will I rub him?" I lifted her up but the pony was out of reach. We talked to the pony for a second and then I persuaded her that we had to return home. I told her that Grandfather was going to buy her a pony. She is delighted at this and seems content at the prospect that one morning she will wake up and find a pony in her field. "Daddy," she said as we got back in the car, "Grandfather buy my pony." "That's right Deirdre, if you're a very very good girl . . . and sit still until we get home."

The peace of Glencolumbkille is as old as history. In the sixth century, St. Columba, also known as Colmcille, is said to have retreated with his disciples here, away from the world. According to tradition, on arriving in the glen and finding numerous pagan standing stones, the saint, a descendant of the Irish king, Niall of the Nine Hostages, relentlessly went about converting them to Christian use, having crosses and emblems carved on the stones and inaugurating a penitential pilgrimage or turas around them.

This turas is still performed in Glencolumbkille today, especially on June 9, St. Columba's feast day. With Deirdre walking between us, we set off with a small map to follow some of the stops around the valley. They were each marked with small white signposts in fields off the side of the road, and to each of them belonged a particular rite of prayer. Had we been completing the pilgrimage proper, we should have gone barefoot over the three miles or so, passed each station on the left and circled, praying, three times. But our aim that afternoon, between the showers, was simply to walk to some of these special places of Columba with Deirdre.

At the first station was a tall, weathered, round-topped standing stone with Celtic markings carved on it. It had been standing there forever it seemed, had stood the test of time, and would be standing there, I imagined, to the end of time itself. We left the first station and headed off for Áit na nGlún, the Place of the Knees. Swirls of mist were moving along the mountaintops on either side of us. A fisherman coming home passed us on the road and nodded. We were walking along a route that had been traveled in prayer for fourteen hundred years. At Áit na nGlún, our leaflet told us, while the pilgrim knelt at the small cavity in the ground, a loose stone from the cairn was passed around the pilgrim's body. At Station 5, the ruins of Colmcille's Chapel, was a slab called Colmcille's Bed upon which pilgrims lay performing the station, seven Hail Marys, seven Our Fathers, seven Glorias, and the Creed. Three yards to the east was another slab, the Flagstone of the Request, standing upon which, facing the valley, traditionally, three requests may be made. Sometimes a handful of clay can be taken from under the stone. This clay, said the leaflet, is said to protect against fire and also holds a cure for headaches and other sickness.

We walked to Colmcille's Chair, Colmcille's Well, and Mullach na Cainte, the Slope of the Conversation, the only place on the three-hour pilgrimage where pilgrims were allowed to speak. As we walked, the mists hovered in the glen and became a veil of rain so fine and white that the fields rising on the mountain's slope vanished from sight. Drenched in the peace of the place—and the rain—we turned back toward the village.

To Chris and me the spirit of St. Columba seemed still, in some way, to survive. There is a feeling of retreat from the world in this valley between the mountains and the sea. As we came away from the turas I reminded myself that it was only two days since we had been in Clare.

We stopped for tea in the tea shop at the Folk Village. We sat at one of the long wooden tables set up for the visitors and sipped our tea beneath a large framed photograph of the other key spirit of Glencolumbkille, Father James McDyer.

He is one of a handful of rural Irish priests of almost mythic stature. While sometimes thought of as a socialist and a radical, he was a figure who had become so closely associated with this place that people in the rest of the country often referred to him as Father McDyer of Glencolumbkille. He was a Donegal man. Moved from his position of curate on Tory Island off the Donegal coast, he came to Glencolumbkille in 1951 at the age of forty-one. The place he arrived in suffered from five curses: no electricity, no industry, no public water supply, unsurfaced roads, and no dispensary. Emigration was widespread. Over the course of the following thirty-five years, Father McDyer dedicated himself to restoring pride to the people of one of the most beautiful valleys in Ireland. A list of dates from his life comprises a history of achievement: 1953, community hall opened; 1954, electricity switched on and first factory opened; 1955, first phase of road improvements; 1956, first piped water scheme and the revival of Irish music festivals and competitions; 1962, first co-op factory opened; 1964, hand-knitting cooperative started; 1964, group water schemes; 1966, knitting factory opened; 1967, folk museum opened; 1970, development association formed and craft shop opened in Dublin; 1971, hotel bought, extended in 1973 and fully modernized by 1978.

After two decades of heady progress, the Glencolumbkille Development Cooperative finally came to an end. It was decided in 1980 that the cooperative should sell its assets and place them in a trust fund for the future development and needs of the community. Before he died in 1987, Father McDyer wrote his autobiography. In it he described his years in Glencolumbkille, and in writing of the future of the parish, he hoped no visitor to Glencolumbkille would ever be irritated or bothered "by money-making gimmickry at every corner," for what people wanted, he believed, were indigenous crafts and musical entertainments that reflected the cultural traditions of a place.

So what of Glencolumbkille two years after his death? In July and August, there are set-dancing classes and through the summer week-long holidays for adults wishing to learn or improve their Irish. There was an archeological week and a fiddlers' festival. In a loose-leaf folder given out by an earnest lady of the Glencolumbkille Tourist Development Committee were leaflets on walks, climbing, swimming, fishing, archeology, arts and crafts, and the flora and fauna of southwest Donegal. Not a mile from our house there was a knitwear factory at Malinmore where, in a low white building, fifteen people were employed, eight of them from the same family.

From our vantage point beneath Father McDyer's photograph, we could read the quotations of his that were displayed alongside his photograph, and they rang out with the idealism of the sixties and the passionate single-mindedness of the valley's saint, whose will had transformed stone pagan slabs to Christian monuments.

The frontiers of God's family do not end with the walls of our home, but extend to the perimeter of the community to which we belong. 1962

The political parties have turned the land into a battlefield where self-interest takes priority over party, and party takes priority over the common good. If anything is for the common good, let not cynicism, criticism or frustration stand in the way. 1966

Let us not cease our sacrifices and endeavours until the agony of emigration, the pinch of penury, and the slur of indolence shall have been lifted from the brows of men. 1966.

Once in Donegal, take any route, stop anywhere, take any side road and you are on your way into a kind of fantasyland. The landscape of this most northern part of the Republic is remarkably dramatic because of its coastal views and mountains. Mick O'Neill, an old friend from my schooldays in Dublin, now working in Donegal, had been visiting. We set off from Glencolumbkille in the early morning to drive him back to Kerrykeel on Mulroy Bay. Fifteen minutes beyond the village and we were at the green houseless sweep of the Glengesh Pass, the road a gray thread weaving down in the distance between the slopes of two mountains. Talking of how people perceive beauty differently, Chris read Thomas Carlyle's opinion of the pass: "Moor, moor, brown heather and peatpot, here and there a speck reclaimed into bright green and the poor cotter gone. Ragged sprawling bare farmstead . . . no hedge or tree— ugly enough." We thought it beautiful. At the foot of the pass was the hillside village of Ardara, a center of Donegal knitwear and tweed. Beyond the village we drove into the wild landscape once more. A mile beyond Ardara the road was again empty and windy, a sweep of grays and browns, of the blooming heather, looking purple by the roadside and reddish brown on the mountains. A length of Donegal tweed under a changing sky.

Here in Donegal had been the domain of the legendary Hugh O'Donnell, one of the great sixteenth-century chieftains, of whom it was written in the Annals of the Four

Masters, "His countenance was so beautiful that everyone who looked upon him loved him. He was perfectly proportioned, very strong and well set in figure, of middle height, rather tall than short. His complexion was that clear brightness which usually accompanies red hair, and his eyes, full, grey, and luminous, and keen as an eagle's." Joining forces with the armies of Hugh O'Neill of Tyrone, O'Donnell had led a winter march the length of the country to what was to become one of the most fateful battles in Irish history. At Kinsale in Cork on Christmas Day 1601, the forces of the Irish chieftains were soundly routed by an English army under the command of Mountjoy; O'Neill and O'Donnell fled to exile in what became romantically known as the Flight of the Earls. The plantation of Ulster with English and Scottish families began. Yet Irish is still more widely spoken here than in any other county, and with Donegal's strange mountainy geography, bordering Northern Ireland and the sea, with only the narrow bridge of land to Sligo and the Republic, it was easy to feel the county was almost an island.

From Ardara to Glenties, from Glenties up to Dungloe, capital of the area known as The Rosses, we drove. Gray skies, lowering rain, small rushy lakes with little waves slapping, miles and miles of stretching boglands, the road lined with telephone poles all the way to the mountains on the horizon. We motored on saying nothing, driving northward, the only car in sight.

At Gweedore we turned right for Gortahork instead of heading for Bloody Foreland (named for its spectacular red sunsets, red sand stone, and red heather) because the sky had fallen. Great showers lashed down and then half cleared to show the cold white quartzite cone of Mount Errigal, Donegal's highest mountain, sitting in every northward view like some leftover fragment of the Ice Age. At Falcarragh we reached the northern coastline. Years previously, Chris and I had turned off the road up here at a hand-made sign saying "Trá," which in Irish means beach. We had driven down the road two miles or so, and arrived eventually at a bank of dunes. Climbing over them, we had come out on what we thought was the longest, most beautiful beach in the world. Surf crashed in long rolling waves against a golden white strand. There was absolutely nobody there. On that never-ending stretch of sand and sea we had run about in the wild wind as if in a secret world. Even though it had been windy and cold, we lay down wrapped in our coats to sleep. Afterward, we could never quite pin down on the map just where we had been.

Now, heading on the road for Dunfanaghy, we saw the same sign: "Trá." I stopped the car and looked over at Chris. Would we chance finding it again? Chris has talked repeatedly about this beach and I knew she wanted to rediscover it. Deirdre was asleep beside her in the backseat. She smiled and nodded and I reversed. Mick wondered what we were conspiring about.

"A beach." I mouthed the words silently.

"A beach?" he said. "There are dozens of beaches just north of us." North Donegal was full of the cleanest, emptiest, most beautiful beaches in Ireland he told us.

"But not like this one, Mick," Chris whispered. Mick shrugged his shoulders and I drove farther along the side road, past a line of houses and farmyards, a junction. Right or left? I turned left.

"I think it was right," Chris said.

After a couple of minutes and no sign of the beach, I

turned back. Mick was beginning to look at us as if we had just gone mad. Back to the junction then and a turn to the right. Still no sea, and yet we knew it was just there beyond the rise somewhere.

"Is any of this familiar to you?" I asked Chris.

"Well, sort of . . . yes, I think so, I think it's down here."

The road came to a sudden end in a small empty square of concrete with high dunes behind it. We emerged from the car into a blustery seawind. The rain had stopped. We zippered up our rain jackets and, with Deirdre in our arms and Mick following, walked out through a gap in the dunes to see the ocean. Coming through that gap was like coming through the gates of memory.

"This is it!" Chris yelled, taking Deirdre in her arms, kicking off her shoes, and running out onto the beach. Mick and I came trotting after. And there, framed between the jagged coastline of Tory Island on the left and the jutting mound of Horn Head on the right, was that truly magnificent beach, stretching away as far as the eye could see. On the shoreline the blue sea pounded with high breakers crashing whitely to where Chris and Deirdre waited barefoot to meet them. This was a beach at the beginning of the world, I thought. For here on these printless windblown sands was the untouched wild beauty of the earth and sea, unspoiled. This is what Ireland offers. The power and peace of this kind of beauty is more inspiring than anything. We watched Deirdre run across the sand, and smiled.

Is it possible for the wind to blow in one direction and the clouds to run in the other? The clothes on the line are waving madly northeastward and yet the clouds above me seem to be moving southeastward. Maybe the weather is continuously moving in a circle right above us so the rain has no choice but to fall. Everywhere we go in Glencolumbkille people are already reminiscing about the summer we just had. It seems they had "the good weather" up here, too. But we're having rain. I've been waiting all week to take a photo of Glen Head with a spot of sun sparkling on it. Viridian green water crashes against it; the land is the color of light chrome green. The purple moorgrass has changed color and is now orange, making the hills in the distance look like the soft fuzzy skin of unripe apricots. Sheep are everywhere. Deirdre sings, "Mary had a little sheep."

There is so much color here and so many flowers. We were out walking, collecting wildflowers for the house to make it look cheerful. I taught Deirdre the names of them all: white yarrow, everlasting, blue harebells, meadowsweet, purple knapweed, purple loosestrife, and devil's bit and sheep's bit, two flowers that look just like field scabious to me, one tiny blue one, that looks like an alpine plant, and one lilac.

I wonder what Deirdre makes of all this. Does she see what I see? Will she remember any of this holiday? I am looking forward to bringing her back here at the end of another summer to point everything out to her again. Will she recall this? If nothing else, will she recognize a feeling of happiness and peace and say to herself, "I've been here before in this beautiful place where flowers grow by the seaside."

In the gray afternoons (for we remained unlucky with the weather) we sometimes took out the bikes for short damp spins, to the small cove beach at Malinbeg, where down at the bottom of the 149 steps Deirdre played on the sand in her raincoat and swimsuit, and paid no heed to the absence of the sun. Back the three miles then to hot baths and a seat before the fire. To open the door at night was to see nothing at all and to hear only the constant sounds of the sea. Yet this wet loneliness was comforting. One afternoon, driving the few miles away to the shore at Port, through endless acres of bog silvered with light on rainwater, we came out on another cove, this one with white stones, and sat and just watched the rough water. These sea-rapt moments in time would stay with us. I will recall moments of stillness, beauty, and peace: the view at Glen Head, the mists around the turas, and that afternoon sitting with Chris and Deirdre by the white stones at Port.

.   .   .

In Kiltumper the days have become fresher now. Another season's wind scatters the leaves from the sycamore trees around the haybarn and reveals to us, at this high window where we write, the hill fields of Tumper once more. Around the farm there are other signs of the year's end: the reek of turf has already begun to diminish at one corner, the last of the flowers — the dahlias and asters, penstemons and montbretia — color the garden in autumnal shades of red, purple, and yellow. The potatoes are being dug, the onions lifted, and Chris is already planning the movement of overgrown shrubs and perennials to a new shrubbery at the back of the house next spring.

The animals have been moved down from the hill fields to the "fort" field where they will stay until we wean the calves. We have sold two Limosin yearlings and purchased from Michael Downes a heifer that will calve in early spring. We have made our compost and have ordered the sand and flagstones for our winter garden project. In late September Michael Dooley helped us hang a new gate into the half-acre haggard field at the back of the house. Chris rebuilt the stone wall around it and a sheltered paddock now nestles between lines of ash and pine trees.

Endings and beginnings. With another season upon us a new stage of our life here is beginning in the paddock field at the back of the house. Perhaps it was his boyhood memory of horses at Kiltumper that had prompted Chris's grand-father, an immigrant Irishman in New York, to join the army and end up as a major in the cavalry. Thanks to the generosity of Joe and Polly, the tradition of keeping horses that had once been so strong here will be revived.

An arrangement had, more or less, been made between Burke's Riding School in Newmarket-on-Fergus and ourselves. Chris would continue taking riding lessons there and Kevin Burke would be on the lookout for a suitable horse for us. Polly had said that what we needed for our "first" horse was a nice nine-year-old gelding, a family horse, not too big and very quiet. All summer Chris rode steadily at Burke's and Kevin looked out for the kind of horse that we wanted. We were anxious to get one but a little nervous, too, although we had come a long way since that day, five summers ago, when Betsy the cow stampeded and terrified us, leaving us ashamed of our "greenness."

I brought Deirdre one day to watch Chris riding. At first she was stunned by the sight—her mother, tall in the saddle—but then she quickly began to laugh and wave as Chris circled the ring. Going home in the car afterward she had held imaginary reins and instructed herself, up down, up down, kick, just as Kevin had instructed Chris. Deirdre bounced up and down on the backseat until we reached Kilmihil.

Kevin, as they say in Clare, is a fine cool man. In the yard at Burke's he had given me *my* first lesson: "Sit on that box there, sit down. Put your feet forward, now get up. You see you want to put your feet back, that's the way to sit on a horse, feet back like that, heels down, that's good, that's very good." I had stood up from the box and he had nodded. "You'll be fine," he said. "I've six Pan Ams coming at two, six Pan Ams, you didn't see any sign of 'em? No sign of 'em on the road?" I hadn't, I said, only slowly realizing he meant air hostesses. He hurried away to get horses ready and I sat down on the box, put my feet back and stood up again—surprisingly not feeling like a perfect fool. When he gave Chris a leg up and she swung herself over the saddle, Kevin jokingly said, "Ye'll have to buy me along with the horse." How could we not trust such a man? We did. One fall afternoon he told us he'd found us a horse. And when we went to see it, we knew at once that this was the animal for Kiltumper.

Chris named him Malachi, after an ancient Irish king. And Malachi's first rider was Deirdre, held by us both as she sat high up in the saddle for a little walk around the haggard.

With the winter drawing on, our jaunts for this year are over. We have found that the "Irish feeling" is alive and well—from Mrs. Hazlitt's guest house in Belfast to Bonnie Reina's Slea Head House in Dingle, from Ostan Inis Oirr in Aran to Bunratty Castle, from Lacken House in Kilkenny to Bantry House on Bantry Bay, from the shrine at Knock to Glencolumbkille.

This is our Ireland! A country of beauty, a country for children. Our most frequent response to the beauty of the landscape is: imagine childhood here. For Ireland is still a place largely unspoiled, an island in the rain where a great number of children can still live in nature, kick footballs in cow fields, and walk quiet roads to two-room schools. Standards of education are high here. As we have crossed and recrossed the country, we have found there is a connection between the peacefulness, the sense of safety in western villages, the gleeful cries of children at play, growing up in the green shadow of a Kerry mountain or by the pounding sands of an Atlantic shore and our deepest feelings for what Ireland is.

We found another Ireland, too. This is a country from

which 46,000 people, mostly young men and women, have emigrated this year alone. It is a country wavering between growth and decline with entire western villages depleted of their young people. An island country looking inward on itself in a last effort to revitalize industry and create jobs, and outward to its lost children who seek prosperity in America and England and Germany. A poor country facing the dissolution of European trade borders in 1992, fearing that free market enterprise may disable the Irish economy. A country that sometimes seems wrapped in a perpetual shawl of grief, variously woven of emigration, high unemployment, and the "Troubles" of Ulster. The Belfast we had found so friendly had nervously commemorated the twentieth anniversary of the arrival of British troops in the North. In Rathfriland, not far from the Brontë Homeland Drive, a Catholic man was shot at his front door—and the suspected murderers were members of the Ulster Defence Regiment security force. This, too, is Ireland.

In her bright blue Wellies, Deirdre has taken to coming with Chris and me after breakfast down the Kiltumper road to check on our cows. The bumpy curving road along the farm's edge has become familiar to her; she knows our fields, our gates, and our cows, and walks alongside us with a knowledgeable air. Two autumns previously, we remember wheeling her, jostling her pram down the same road and picking her first blackberries from the great tangle of fruit bushes that grow high and wild by the roadside. A year ago she had half walked and been half carried, but she had been able to spot and demand the berries herself, so that we had often hurried her past them to get home. Now, in her third autumn on the Kiltumper road, she stops, walks to the blackberry bushes herself, and carefully picks the ripest ones, walking on with us smiling gleefully with a purple-stained mouth. This is and will always be "Deirdre's blackberry road" now. Everyday in coming back from the cows and turning in the gate we see the quickening of Deirdre's step on the road as she runs in to check the hiding places where the hens leave their eggs. She finds two and brings them carefully the rest of the way to the house beside us. We all three take off our Wellies and leave them inside the back door. "Ráite fó foiss fogamar," autumn is an excellent season for staying at home. Or, as Deirdre says, "Home again, home again, jiggedy jig."

Niall Williams was born and raised in Dublin. He has an M.A. in American literature from University College Dublin and a Certificate in Farming from the Irish Agricultural Advisory Board.

Christine Breen was born in New Jersey and grew up in suburban Westchester County, New York. She is a graduate of Boston College and has an M.A. in Irish literature from U.C.D., where she was studying when she met Niall. They were wed in 1981.

They worked in publishing in New York before deciding to become small farmers. They live now in the cottage in which Christine's grandfather was born near the village of Kilmihil in County Clare.

Together they have written *O Come Ye Back to Ireland, When Summer's in the Meadow,* and *The Pipes Are Calling* telling of their lives in Ireland.